WHAT YOU AREN'T SEEING

WHAT YOU AREN'T SEEING

How Using Your Hidden Potential Can Help You Discover the Leader Within

THE INSPIRING STORY OF

HERB GREENBERG

BY PATRICK SWEENEY

New York Chicago San Francisco Athens London Madrid
Mexico City Milan New Delhi Singapore Sydney Toronto

1 2 3 4 5 6 7 8 9 0   DOC/DOC   1 2 1 0 9 8 7 6 5

ISBN   978-0-07-184975-3
MHID   0-07-184975-0

e-ISBN   978-0-07-184976-0
e-MHID   0-07-184976-9

Library of Congress Cataloging-in-Publication Data
Sweeney, Patrick, 1952-
    What you aren't seeing : how using your hidden potential can help you discover the leader within / Patrick Sweeney.
        pages cm
    ISBN 978-0-07-184975-3 (alk. paper) — ISBN 0-07-184975-0 (alk. paper)
    1. Leadership—Psychological aspects. 2. Leadership. I. Title.
    BF637.L4.S94 2015
    158'.4—dc23
                                                                            2015009279

McGraw-Hill Education books are available at special quantity discounts to use as premiums and sales promotions, or for use in corporate training programs. To contact a representative, please visit the Contact Us page at www.mhprofessional.com.

Contents

At the age of nine, Herb had a serious operation. Then, because of an infection, over the next year, spots started to appear before his eyes and he slowly, without realizing what was going on, lost his sight.

Psychological Insights—Trust: You realize just how important trust is when you walk with someone who is blind. Where's the wall? Is there a curb? Are you sure you're paying close enough attention, watching out for both of you?

Questions to Ask Yourself: Whom do you trust? Who trusts you? Can you rebuild trust?

After losing his sight, over the course of the next year, Herb and his parents alternately challenged and accepted what had happened. There were certain things they would accept and others that they would not.

Psychological Insights—Resilience: Where does strength in the face of adversity come from? How can you develop it? When all is said and done, resilience has a lot to do with defining who you are.

Questions to Ask Yourself: What can you accept? What can you not accept? Are you clear on what you will fight for?

Attending school in the heart of Bedford-Stuyvesant, one of Brooklyn's toughest areas, Herb would get attacked daily. To this day, he always has his right hand free so he can swing if he is attacked, though he has not been in a fight since he was 13.

Psychological Insights—Grit and Flow: What is the connection between flow, a state of being where everything seems effortless, and grit, the ability to passionately and persistently pursue a long-term goal?

Questions to Ask Yourself: When was the last time you gave your all to anything? What would you like to give your all to now?

SECTION 2 | Seeing New Possibilities

From an early age, Herb was instilled with a strong sense that he always had to be "just a little better" because of his disability. With that motivation, despite enormous odds, he received his Ph.D. with highest honors from New York University at the age of 25.

Psychological Insights—Courage: We often think of courageous people as being totally fearless. But courage really involves feeling fear, facing it head-on, then moving beyond it. Courage is about standing up for ourselves, for others, or for a belief.

Questions to Ask Yourself: Do you have any hesitations about questioning authority? What happens when you become the authority? Do you forget to ask those tough questions?

After Herb received his Ph.D., when his potential employers found out that he was blind, he received no job offers. "Now that was rejection," he says.

Psychological Insights—Goal-Oriented: Before setting a goal, you need to be clear about what you really want—not what others want for you or what you believe is expected of you.

Questions to Ask Yourself: Do negative messages affect you more than positive ones? What new challenge are you primed for?

With $15,000 borrowed and an embryonic idea about helping people identify and realize their potential, Herb and his partner tried to make their mark. Just as they were running out of funds, an executive from General Motors decided to take a chance on them.

Psychological Insights—Persuasiveness: Understanding where people are coming from can help you bring them along willingly, rather than pushing them. If you start pushing, they'll either push back or you'll push them away.

Questions to Ask Yourself: When you are trying to persuade people, where do you start? How do you know they are ready to be open with you?

SECTION 3 | Seeing Far and Wide

As they offered companies a new way to hire top performers, Herb and his partner found themselves turned away from places where they thought they would be welcomed, then, occasionally, when they least expected it, surprised by an opportunity that would open like a skyline.

Psychological Insights—Taking Risks: At the end of the day, we can calculate a risk all we want to. But then some of us will take it, while others will take a pass.

Questions to Ask Yourself: What is the biggest risk you've ever taken in your career? What is the biggest risk you've ever taken in your personal life? Do you think about those two risks differently?

"For better or worse," Herb says, "I have never been completely satisfied. At least, not for too long. I am always feeling that there is more to be done, more we can do. I guess that created a dynamic where I was always trying to be just 'a little better.'"

> *Psychological Insights—Never Being Satisfied:* "I just have to keep constantly moving forward," Herb says. "Always finding new journeys. Because I cannot settle. I don't have the slightest interest in settling. Not in the least. It is not in my nature. And I can't settle for anything less."

> *Questions to Ask Yourself:* Do you keep challenging yourself? When are you satisfied? When are you not satisfied?

Helping anyone who is in any way disadvantaged is at the core of who Herb is. Between 1968 and 1970, through his in-depth approach to understanding an individual's potential, he helped over 4,000 people move from welfare to work for the first time in their lives.

> *Psychological Insights—Optimism:* Pessimists, essentially, believe that negative things that happen are personal, permanent, and pervasive. Optimists, meanwhile, view positive things that happen the same way—as personal, permanent, and pervasive.

> *Questions to Ask Yourself:* What are you standing for? What are you standing against?

"It was a very exciting time," Herb recalls. "I remember sitting on a Boeing 707 with a publicist we brought over for the occasion, and he kept marveling, 'We're going to where Shakespeare lived.'"

> *Psychological Insights—Urgency:* "As it turns out," Herb reflects, "one of my main faults might also be one of my major virtues. This fault, if you will, is that there is just something in me that cannot wait."

> *Questions to Ask Yourself:* What, from your perspective, is so important that it cannot wait? How many things in your life are important *and* urgent?

Leading is about constantly looking within you and around you—being aware of how your strengths can help you (or get in the way) as the marketplace around you continually evolves.

> *Psychological Insights—Entrepreneur:* "Entrepreneurs know that they could be making a huge mistake with each and every move," Herb says. But they also know that they could be making a bigger mistake by not making a move.

> *Questions to Ask Yourself:* Under what circumstances do you wish you were more assertive? With what people do you wish you were more assertive?

While he could not help the Brooklyn Dodgers, Herb's insights have helped over three dozen professional sports teams—from baseball to basketball to football to hockey—with their draft choices.

Psychological Insights—Competitiveness: People who are competing with themselves will continually try to improve. It's part of who they are. As a leader, those are the individuals you want to surround yourself with.

Questions to Ask Yourself: Who are you really competing with? Yourself? Or someone else?

While pursuing an opportunity, Herb uncovered more than he had bargained for. Through an in-depth study, he developed a model of leadership that has had enormous implications for how leaders need to adapt in order to be effective in today's global marketplace.

Psychological Insights—Control: Understanding control—what we can control and what we cannot—is vital for leaders. By its nature, control comes with many inherent contradictions, if not illusions.

Questions to Ask Yourself: What are your top three leadership qualities? How can you enhance those qualities?

"We know that we could no longer avoid making some of the most painful decisions that we have ever had to make," Herb says. "In order to get through the eye of this storm, we were going to have to shrink to half our size."

Psychological Insights—Rising to Challenges: "Persevering through this challenging time, when our bank had completely lost faith in our ability to stay afloat, confirmed my core beliefs," Herb says.

Questions to Ask Yourself: What is one of your core beliefs? Have you ever had it tested?

"I want to make Caliper all that it should be," Herb says. "What I want mainly is for Caliper to grow, to be seen, to be appreciated, to make the kind of impact that our philosophy is capable of making."

Psychological Insights—Succession: As a leader, one of your most important responsibilities is to develop future leaders within your organization. That starts with being able to recognize someone else's potential—which, in many ways, is like trying to see into the future.

Questions to Ask Yourself: Do you know the next step in your leadership journey? Do you know who could replace you in your current position? Have you been grooming him or her?

CHAPTER 18 **What's Your Story?**

Your leadership story is what illuminates you, making you known, understood, and worth following. Ultimately, your story defines you as a leader. It tells others where you are from, where you are going, what you will stand for, and what you will not stand for.

Psychological Insights—Looking Within: As a leader, others are looking for you to be genuinely, rigorously, and continually trying to improve. Are you ready to keep getting ready?

Questions to Ask Yourself: What would you like a child to learn from your life? How will you lead differently today than you did yesterday? What do you want to do tomorrow?

CONCLUSION **The Next Step**

As a leader, or future leader, you will be able to take advantage of a unique gift to help you discover your defining qualities. As a reader of this book you will be able to take Caliper's in-depth personality profile at no cost and receive a developmental guide that pinpoints the qualities that distinguish you and gives suggestions for developing your potential.

Preface

Your leadership journey
starts with your story.

Leading is all about connecting.

In order for others to follow you, they need, first and foremost, to connect with you. They have to trust you. They need to know where you are from so they can believe in you. Only then can they have confidence that you will be able to load them where they need to go.

That is why they yearn, above all else, to know your story.

Your story is what connects where you are from with where you are going. It conveys what you will and what you will not stand for. It opens the door to who you are—so that others can believe in you. Your story connects you more deeply with yourself and with those around you.

With that in mind, as Herb Greenberg's story unfolds, I encourage you to think about the spirit and meaning of your own story. What is it that drives you? What are your unique qualities? Is it your passion? Or your compassion? Your vision of the future? Or your connection with the past? Your sheer determination? Or your ability to collaborate? Your ability to overcome seemingly insurmountable odds? Or your talent for inspiring others?

Throughout Herb's story, you will hear certain themes that repeat themselves and come alive, helping to define him in ways that we can all easily connect with and admire. As you will see in the opening chapter, for instance, Brooklyn is not just a place where Herb grew up, but it is at the core of his identity. It is where the Dodgers infused him with a sense of moxie, as well as a belief in the underdog and the notion that "there will always be next season." Then, in time, the Brooklyn Bridge took him to places he could never have imagined.

As you learn about Herb's inspiring story, I hope it motivates you to think about your own story in a new way. What are the overarching themes of *your* story? What scenes from your life bring those messages alive? How do your personal stories connect with your leadership journey?

To the extent that your leadership story clearly reflects your core values, and you are able to share your story in a compelling way, others will lean in—and believe in you. That is when your true leadership can take hold.

Leading, ultimately, starts with you, and others, knowing the depth of your story.

What is it about you as a leader that reaches deep inside of you and can reach out to connect with others?

What is your leadership story?

Introduction

Before delving into the story, allow me to share a moment of candor. I have had the great fortune of working closely with Herb Greenberg for over a quarter of a century. He has been a mentor, a business partner, and a friend. We wrote two books together (one a *New York Times* bestseller) and presented our findings at global conferences in Shanghai, London, Paris, Dublin, São Paolo, and Honolulu, among many others. When Herb appointed me president of his management consulting firm in January 2009, as the great recession hit us and our clients with a gale force, together we learned an enormous amount as we guided our company through its most challenging time. After realigning our strategy and creating even stronger bonds with our employees and our clients, we led Caliper into a new era, introducing many innovations.

I have long admired Herb's intelligence, wit, creativity, insights, and sheer determination. I am, admittedly, a fan. So, there is no way I can be totally objective. What I can promise you, however, is to provide a candid insider's view into the inner workings of a tireless entrepreneur, one who knows how to see the bright side of any cloudy situation, one who never seems to be daunted by a challenge, one who senses opportunities where others see confusion, one who wants to level the playing field for anyone who (like himself) did not have an equal opportunity, one whose enthusiasm is contagious, one who is always stretching to be "just a little better," and one who pursues his passions with everything he has—and then some.

I can also promise that you will gain insights into the psychological makeup of a leader—insights that you will be able to apply to your own personal leadership journey and that will help you uncover and develop the leadership potential of others. As I tell this story in segments, then step back and provide psychological insights for you to reflect upon, I believe you will find a way to strengthen your own leadership potential so that it convincingly highlights your strengths, beliefs, and values.

What This Book Can Do for You

This book combines an entrepreneur's inspiring personal story with practical ideas and insights that can help you become the leader you were meant to be.

Herb Greenberg, who lost his sight at the age of 10, has been able to see something that many of us inadvertently overlook—our own potential, and the potential of those around us.

He went on to create a consulting firm with offices in over a dozen countries that for more than a half century has helped Fortune 500 companies as well as start-ups and organizations in-between to discover and develop the potential of their applicants and employees.

This book was created to share insights from Herb's inspiring story, with the goal of helping you realize your own leadership potential, uncover the potential of those around you, and see a new world of possibilities.

In the rendering of this unique story, you will find three distinct interwoven layers. On one level, there is a truly inspirational success story about an entrepreneur who faces daunting challenges with fervent belief, hope, and confidence. In parallel, we will delve into psychological qualities derived from this story so that you can reflect upon how you might apply these insights for yourself and others. In addition, each chapter contains questions for you to consider as you create your own vision, tap into your personal strengths, pursue your own leadership journey, and seek to develop leaders around you.

Herb's story is about overcoming seemingly insurmountable odds, finding an inner strength, connecting with others, creating his own path, loving what he does, and succeeding on his own terms. His lessons will resonate viscerally with the hearts and minds of leaders everywhere. Essential to his story, as it is for every leader, is knowing what to accept and, equally important, knowing what to fight for.

I am very enthused about sharing this story because inside of it, I believe you may also glean psychological insights into how you as a leader can shape your own story, sense opportunities, become more optimistic, overcome rejection, take necessary risks, strive to be "just a little bit better," and see new possibilities in yourself and in those with whom you choose to surround yourself.

With that, there is one last thing I can promise: the story of a leader that will engage and inspire you—touching your heart and opening your mind.

Seeing Inside Yourself

Are You Connecting?

Whenever people talk about Herb's accomplishments, they invariably end with the same sentiment.

And it makes him cringe.

Certainly, many are impressed to meet an icon in the world of psychological assessments, one who codeveloped an approach that can accurately identify an individual's strengths, motivations, and potential. Their thoughts may have been expanded by one of the articles he coauthored in the *Harvard Business Review*, just as their hearts may have been touched by a keynote presentation he delivered at a global conference. But invariably, they end by saying something along the lines of *"and, on top of all that, he is blind."*

That last sentiment is very unsettling for Herb. He dislikes it. Immensely.

"It makes me extremely uncomfortable," he says, definitively. *"The truth is that everyone has some kind of disability, and it does* frustrate me that I can't do certain things I know I would have enjoyed, like playing tennis. I love sports, and I would have loved to have played on a team. But my disability ruled that out. I'd love to see a beautiful woman. I would also love to scuba dive and see all the multicolored fish. These are things I miss. The reality is that being blind can be limiting and annoying. After getting my Ph.D. with highest honors, I was denied certain jobs because I was blind. When I was a teenager, there were certain girls who wouldn't go out with me because I was blind. Sometimes their parents wouldn't let their daughters go out with me because of my blindness. All that hurt. It really hurt."

As he reflected on how he had been rejected by some simply because he was blind, the psychologist in him considered how "rejection can paralyze some people, while causing others to carry on with even more determination."

Herb is less interested in focusing on the differences that some people may use to stereotype or limit others, and more interested in uncovering the strengths inside of each of us that can distinguish us and create enormous possibilities.

His life's work has been about trying to establish a level playing field where the potential of each of us can be identified and developed, making all the difference in the world.

He has a soft spot for the underdog, for those who have not been given an equal and fair shot simply because of prejudice—about their gender, their race, or any preconceived "disability."

Still, it is an intriguing paradox. Something that others admire about him, at a level that they find truly astonishing, he finds to be a nuisance, a burden, something he'd prefer to skip over, like a stone that a child flicks across a lake. Rather than being known as someone who overcame, at momentous levels, the disadvantages of being blind, Herb would like to be known as someone from Brooklyn who, with an extra dash of moxie, took a shot, and continues to keep taking shot after shot after shot.

His Anchor and His Bridge

When you get to know Herb, he often starts by talking about where he's from. Brooklyn is where he started and, at least in his mind, always returns; it is his anchor and his bridge. Brooklyn is where he got his determination, his way of seeing the world, and his very identity.

By way of a quick example, several years ago, as we sat waiting to interview Senator Barbara Boxer (D-CA), who also grew up in Brooklyn, for our book *Succeed on Your Own Terms*, I leaned over to Herb and whispered, "Listen, I know you love to reminisce about your old stomping grounds, but could you just hold off on it this once? We have a lot to cover, with very little time to do it in."

"Sure. No problem," he assured me, as the senator walked into the room. She greeted us warmly, then immediately said she had heard that Herb was from Brooklyn. And there was nothing I could do. In a New York minute, they both dove into the deep end of reminiscing. When two people from Brooklyn first meet, and I've come to know this pattern, they play a game where they first name streets and places. (It's like a test, as if someone might actually fake being from Brooklyn.) So, the senator and Herb started talking about where you could get the best cheesecake in the world (Junior's, of course); then Ebbets Field, where the Dodgers would always come back next year; and finally, the section of Brooklyn where she grew up (Borough Park), and the section where he grew up (Crown Heights). And while all of this was going on, I was thinking, "I don't believe this. A half hour is almost up, and all I've got from this interview is reminiscences about the bridge, the Dodgers, and Coney Island." Then, just as they were about to promise to meet at Nathan's for a hot dog, one of the senator's assistants poked his head in, saying that they had to rush off to their next appointment.

I *knew* it. I could sense this coming a mile away. Our time was up. All I had was a recording of two people from Brooklyn agreeing that there was no place better to grow up. I was empty-handed, our time had elapsed, and my options were gone.

Then the most unexpected thing happened, as the senator held up her hand and said she wanted to continue this interview, instructing her assistant to push her schedule back an hour. And just like that, the conversation shifted gears. The senator began covering both personal and professional ground, speaking with enormous candor about her hopes, disappointments, and sense of history. Her insights, as well as some of her memories about growing up in Brooklyn, became one of the key chapters in our book about believing in yourself and pursuing your dreams.

———————

This meeting illustrates a key quality of Herb's, and it is one that runs the risk of becoming a lost art form. *In a world of tweets, texts, and sound bites, I've often been struck by Herb's ability to immediately connect with people. His formula for engaging with others is simple and straightforward. His conversations quickly become personal and meaningful, leading to deep relationships.*

"Generally speaking, my approach is just to want to connect," he explained. "If you are genuinely interested in someone else, they usually respond in kind. It's just about being interested. We all like to get a smile. So, I like to start off by giving one. And it is usually returned. When I first meet someone, I talk with them *as if* we were friends. That's my assumption. Why not? Then, through acting as if we are friends, we become friends very quickly."

———————

Alyson Brandt, president USA at Fusion Learning, said she has viewed Herb as a mentor throughout her entire professional career. "I met him when I was just starting in the business world," she noted. His advice enabled me to feel the confidence I needed to jump full force into becoming a sales professional. And I have turned to him at every important stage in my career: from becoming a global sales leader to now being at the helm of U.S. operations for a global learning company." She describes Herb as having "enthusiasm that is off the charts, along with a quick mind, advice that is wise and focused, and a wonderful mix of drive, vision, and playfulness."

"Herb, first and foremost, has this tremendous smile and a positive vibe about him that is contagious," added Tom Gartland, the former president, North America for Avis Budget Group. "He has this extremely positive aura, with an energy so high that it just completely blows me away. His memory is uncanny, his insights profound, and he connects with people in a way that is genuine, positive, and inspirational."

Laura Kohler, senior vice president of human resources at Kohler Co., agreed completely, describing Herb as "an expert with an entrepreneurial spirit, who is very warm and passionate, and has a remarkable way of drawing people into him and establishing trust."

What does he look for, and what does he try to convey when he initially meets someone?

In a "Forethought Conversation" in the *Harvard Business Review*, Herb was asked, "Do managers overemphasize or misread visual clues when evaluating people for jobs or promotions?" He responded, "Most people depend too much on their sight. How does someone look? Do they fit the part? Some of those visual cues can be as superficial and inaccurate as 'She seems to carry herself like a leader' or 'He looks like he would fit in with the rest of the department.' That first impression then becomes the context for the rest of the information they gather about an individual. They may hear the person's responses differently because they like what they see or because the person is smiling convincingly at them. That's one of the reasons why, during Freudian therapy, an individual is on the couch, facing away from the therapist, who just listens."

When asked, What sorts of nonvisual cues do you notice? Herb responded, "The proverb says, 'The eyes are the window to the soul,' but I think it's the voice. People can work on their smile. They can convey a certain look. There's so much plastic surgery these days that someone can actually buy a certain look. But voices are genuine. You can tell if a person is comfortable with you, not putting up barriers. Or you can tell if there's no reaching out in the person's voice. When someone's voice is flat or quiet, you don't have any idea what he or she is feeling or thinking. That can be a warning flag."

That's why Herb says he makes an extra effort to pay close attention to people's voices. Is there warmth? Genuine enthusiasm? Sincerity? A way of expressing themselves that is real? Or are they trying too hard? Uncomfortable with themselves? Not really interested? Thinking about something else?

Where does his ability to read and authentically connect with people come from?

"I think part of the way I connect with people has to do with how I grew up," Herb says. "We all talked to each other. It was what we did, how we engaged. We were rarely inside on a hot summer day. But if we were, we'd have our windows open, so we might hear the bell ringing from a Bungalow Bar or Good Humor ice cream truck going by. Then we'd all run out with our nickel, buy something, and then sit around talking as we ate our ice cream. Most of the time, though, we were always outside anyway, playing a game or sitting on the stoops and street corners, trying to catch a breeze. So we were always having conversations with our friends and neighbors. It was just part of how we lived. Always ready to start a conversation. Always connecting.

There was a feeling like we were all in it together." He paused, then added, "Nowadays, we stay inside, where the air-conditioning keeps us cool."

And, perhaps, separates us from each other.

Where Do You Start Your Connections?

The ability to truly connect with others, to engage in meaningful conversations, may be one of the most important attributes leaders can learn from their elders. While social media certainly has many advantages—we can now connect faster and in ways that were unimaginable just a few years ago—it is important to recognize that our connections through social media are very different. And it is worth considering that those connections alone may not be engaging us as deeply as we might hope.

In previous generations, we looked to our elders to instill tradition and to pass on wisdom. Now, however, they (and perhaps we, as well) too often feel that their experiences have little to do with our current lives—that the ground beneath them is shifting so quickly that their advice may sound as if it is coming from a completely different world.

As we seek to engage, however, their conversational wisdom, as Herb expresses so clearly, may have much more to teach us than the latest addition to Wikipedia.

How can leaders become more engaged in their professional and personal lives?

Martin Seligman, the founder of positive psychology, offers that to find meaning and true happiness, we all need to have a rich repertoire of friends with whom we stay connected. It is through those connections that the strength of our character is enhanced and we truly flourish.

The last thing in the world we are looking for is another prerecorded phone message, a five-second sound bite, or a 140-character tweet to guide us. We are looking for real conversations with each other, sharing our joys and losses, our depth and meaning.

We are seeking to engage, and to be engaged.

As Herb suggests, the last thing in the world we want to do is backtrack or wish we could set the clock back to a "golden age." Instead, the way to find true engagement may be through finding our own new and unique blend of connecting with each other—one that combines the ubiquity of social media with the intimacy of personal conversations.

Through that enhancement, we may be able to find true engagement on a broad and deep level. And in those engagements, leaders may find what they have been missing in themselves and in those around them.

Can You Hear Me?

Have you ever noticed how people deal with their cell phones differently when they are on a train? Most of them are texting. But those who are talking on their phones invariably start the conversation with something like, "Can you hear me OK?"

They know that the signal strength may be limited or fluctuate as the train is moving. So, with the anticipation of a technical glitch, they naturally ask if their connection is OK.

It is rare, however, that we confirm whether or not we have a strong connection when we are just having a regular conversation with someone. But it might be something worth considering. As leaders, we could probably all benefit from asking, from time to time, how strong our connection is. Is the other person available to listen right now? Can that person give you his or her full attention? Or would there be a better time to try to connect? Are you being clear and open? Or are you losing your signal?

Taking a minute to test out the connection between you and the person you are trying to connect with can go a long way toward increasing the understanding between you and him or her.

An Experiment

Herb commented in the *Harvard Business Review* that he learns an enormous amount about people from listening to the intonation, cadence, and genuineness of their voice. Here's an interesting experiment to try based on this concept.

Try concentrating on people's voices. Do it for a full day. Then ask yourself: Can you describe the voice of someone you genuinely care about? How does he or she make you feel? How does the person's voice add to his or her words?

Now try describing the voice of someone who drives you absolutely crazy. How would you describe that voice? How does it make you feel? How does it take away from the person's words?

Now think about your own voice.

Psychological Insights—Empathy

How do you tune in to others and understand where they are coming from? Herb says, "Empathy is the starting place for succeeding in virtually every relationship—on a professional level as well as in our personal lives."

Having assessed the potential and motivation of more than four million individuals around the world, Caliper's research shows that empathy is actually rarer than you might think.

"Most of us get stuck interpreting the world from our own narrow point of view," Herb says. And that can be very limiting, particularly *as the world becomes smaller, communication happens faster and connections are made—or missed—in a heartbeat.*

We can all express sympathy. When we hear of someone's misfortune, we send a card or say, "I'm very sorry to hear about your loss." But, as Herb pointed out in the *Harvard Business Review*, true empathy starts with making a genuine connection and really being able to understand where another person is coming from.

"It is important to keep in mind that empathy does not necessarily involve agreeing with the feelings of others, but it does involve knowing what their feelings and ideas are," Herb adds.

Empathy is the ability to read others. It's knowing what drives them. It's being able to intuit their strengths, limitations, potential, and motivations. Empathy is the ability to pick up the subtle clues and cues provided by others in order to accurately assess what they are thinking and feeling.

There are three distinct ways individuals can come across as being empathic.

"Individuals who are genuinely empathic have very high levels of *flexibility*, *openness*, and *sensitivity*," Herb says. They have natural warmth, which others immediately sense and respond to. When someone who is empathic asks how others are, they often receive a real, sometimes surprising answer. "We can sense that they care, and as a result, our relationship can become more open and meaningful," he added.

We have also come across individuals who have what we would measure to be a moderate level of empathy, but when the situation calls for it, they are able to turn up the volume on their empathy. And their situational empathy allows them to tune in, when needed, to pick up the subtle clues and cues that others might miss.

"In addition," Herb says, "we have consulted with individuals who succeed because they have a natural intellectual curiosity and are very accommodating. Such individuals can come across as being intrigued by how things work and fascinated to know why things are the way they are. And they can also get people to open up."

The results of understanding others can be very similar for all three of these individuals as long as they are being true to themselves and playing to their natural strengths. All three—those with a deep-seated sense of empathy, those who know how to turn up the volume on the empathy they have, and those who are intellectually curious and accommodating—are able to connect with others, creating a desired level of trust and confidence. "What is important is that they are being genuine, not trying to be something they are not. Someone who is faking it will turn us off in a minute," he adds. We can all sense a fake a mile away.

That being said, we are naturally drawn to people who possess genuine empathy. Empathy is the starting place for connecting.

Ironically, according to Aristophanes, that longing for a true connection with another was a punishment that Zeus cast on the human race. In order to teach us humility, he split us in two. Ever since that day, we have wandered the world, searching for our other halves. It is in that searching, Aristophanes causes us to consider, that we are pursuing our complete self, a sense of wholeness, our well-being.

Clearly, from a leadership perspective, empathy is needed to make real and lasting connections with others. As Daniel Goleman, psychologist and author of *Emotional Intelligence*, wrote, "Executives who can effectively focus on others are easy to recognize. They are the ones who find common ground, whose opinions carry the most weight, and with whom other people want to work. They emerge as natural leaders regardless of organizational or social rank."

Confirming this premise, Claudio Fernández-Aráoz, a senior advisor at global executive search firm Egon Zehnder, found in an analysis of new C-level executives that those who had been hired for their self-discipline, drive, and intellect were sometimes later let go because they lacked social skills. While they were extremely bright and could focus single-mindedly on results, their inability to get along socially on the job led to their professional undoing.

Harvard Business School professor and former CEO of Medtronic Bill George echoes, "Authentic leaders demonstrate a passion for their purpose, practice their values consistently, and lead with their hearts as well as their heads. They establish long-term, meaningful relationships and have the self-discipline to get results." In other words, they know who they are, and they know the strengths and potential of those with whom they decide to surround themselves.

"And it all starts, or stops, with empathy," Herb says.

"Leaders with real empathy are able to connect with those around them in ways that create new openings," he adds. "They are able to make whatever walls may exist between people crumble and disappear. Their empathy is authentic. It all starts with being interested in and caring about others. Genuinely."

Questions to Ask Yourself About Empathy

Below are "a lot of words with question marks after them."
You can view them that way, as something easily skipped
over. Or you can recognize that the questions we ask ourselves determine who we will become. And the most powerful
questions will exceed powerful answers to lesser questions.

These questions are posed for you to consider as you
create your own vision, tap into your personal strengths, and
pursue your own leadership journey. They are to be taken
as seriously as you wish. And they can be taken at different
times, as your answers will undoubtedly evolve and change
as your leadership journey unfolds.

Some of the questions may challenge you. Others may be
among those you've asked yourself from time to time. There
are no right or wrong answers. Only yours. And the extent
to which they change over time is a measure of the degree to
which you are growing as a leader. Your answers to the questions in this section will provide a starting point to consider
the role empathy plays in your approach to leadership.

1. How do you connect with people? Where do you start?
2. When you first meet someone, do you ask questions about
   him or her? Or do you tend to tell the person something about
   yourself first?
3. Do you prefer to start a conversation with someone by talking
   about a light subject? Or do you dive right into something deep
   and meaningful?
4. Do you have a favorite question to ask when you first meet
   someone new?
5. Where do you get inspiration?
6. How often do you smile?
7. How often do you make others smile?
8. What makes you truly happy?

Back to Brooklyn

To get at the heart of the matter, we went back to Brooklyn. (As this leadership journey evolves, keep in mind that, like many stories and certainly most memories, we will not follow an exact linear timeline. Rather, we will traverse places, times, and themes, blending and connecting one with the other with the goal of creating a fuller and richer tapestry.)

As we pulled up, finding a parking place in front of the diner, there was no mistaking this legendary landmark on the corner of DeKalb and Flatbush Avenue extension, with its bright orange awnings and vibrant orange script lettering announcing, as if in a neon memory from days gone by: *Junior's*. Inside, it was easy to imagine that we had been transported back in time as we opened the large glass doors and walked through the bakery section, showcasing strawberry, blueberry, Brooklyn Crumb, and every kind of cheesecake imaginable.

Herb and I slid into one of the bright yellow, green, and orange Naugahyde-upholstered booths, as I described to him how the framed, autographed photos on the walls announced that this was a must-stop eating spot for presidents, movie stars, and, of course, the Brooklyn Dodgers. A waiter in a white shirt with black slacks, vest, and bow tie handed us enormous red-and-white-striped menus that looked like they had not changed since some of the Dodgers first glanced at them nearly seven decades ago. I read highlights from the menu to Herb, including: a mile-long deli sandwich, Tai wings, potato pancake sand-wiches, several kinds of Reubens, Jamaican jerk chicken, mac and cheese pie, Hungarian goulash, fresh brisket of beef, big meatballs with spaghetti, a roasted half-chicken, Virginia ham, baked meatloaf, and Junior's Junior Menu for Your Small Fries. Herb's smile could not have been wider as he said, "Boy, this is *so* Brooklyn!"

We each ordered a slice of chocolate swirl cheesecake and a Fox's U-Bet Brooklyn Chocolate Egg Cream (which has no egg and no cream—just U-Bet syrup, milk, and seltzer) as Herb started to remi-nisce. "Junior's opened in 1950," Herb said. "Prior to that, the same family had a diner here that was not this large and fancy, but was where the Dodgers would come after a game when I was a kid. And you could talk with any of them. All you had to do was buy them a sandwich, a cup of coffee, or a piece of cheesecake. So, when I was just shy of 11 years old, my father was given tickets for us to see the Dodgers play the Giants. My father made custom shoes for the wife of the police inspec-tor in charge of the Polo Grounds, which is where the Giants played, and he was very appreciative and heard that I was a big Dodgers fan."

This was in 1940, a year before the Dodgers would win their first pennant in decades. (For those unfamiliar with Brooklyn, I hesitate to spoil the suspense, but they went on to fall to the New York Yankees in five World Series matches, eventually turning the tide. But we will come to that in due time.) The annual ritual of building hope and expecta-tions, only to lose in a heartbreaking way, became a familiar pattern for long-suffering fans, as "Wait till next year!" became the unofficial slogan of the Dodgers.

For Herb, though, as he was just about to turn 11, this was *his* year. The police inspector not only got tickets for Herb and his father, but they also got to meet some of the players just before the game. "Pee Wee Reese was there," Herb said, "along with Dixie Walker, Dolph Camilli, Fat Freddie Fitzsimmons, and, of course, the manager, Leo Durocher. I could rattle off everyone's name, but they wouldn't mean anything to you."

"Maybe not," I said, "But those are great nicknames. They all sound like they could step right out of a Damon Runyan story."

"They do. Then, referring to me, Pee Wee Reese said, 'This little kid. Would he like to sit in the dugout with us?' And all I remember was nodding, smiling, then letting out a hoot, and saying, 'You bet!' " Herb paused, then added, "And that's how it happened."

Actually being in the dugout, as a little kid, would not have given him the best view of the field, even if he were not blind. (Herb had lost his sight the year before, which we will delve into in just a bit.) But being in the dugout with his heroes gave him much more than a view of the game. What it really gave him was beyond every kid's dream. It wasn't even something he had ever dreamed about. Yet here he was. In the dugout. At the beginning of a game. With his heroes getting ready to make another comeback. He had questions he was dying to ask them about trades that had been made and decisions on the field. But he held back and just savored the experience. Herb had been invited into the inner circle of his favorite team. They were batting, then taking the field. And the innings were flying by. His heroes were all around him, being real, honest, playing with everything they had, playing the game like there was nothing else going on in the world. He got an insider's view of how the team members connected with each other. Meanwhile, he was listening to the broadcast of the game on his little transistor radio. Whenever there was some commotion in the dugout, he would ask what was going on. Generally, Pee Wee Reese was the one who would lean over and explain to Herb what had just happened.

Herb remembers being there when Dolph Camilli hit a home run, and everyone was jumping up and down, screaming. Leaning in to his transistor radio, amid the raucous sounds all around him, Herb could just barely hear Red Barber, who announced the play-by-plays for the Dodgers, say, "Back, back, back." Then, full of excitement, he declared, "It is a Bedford Avenue Blast. We are sitting in the catbird seat."

In those days before television, radio was what everyone gathered around to hear about the outside world. For Herb, though, radio became more than that. It was a lifeline. As a young blind child, he had a special connection to radio. Listening very closely, he learned about sports, politics, and, most particularly, how to tell stories full of color and imagery that tapped into the listener's imagination.

As the players in the dugout were still cheering ecstatically, Camilli leaned down and patted Herb's head. That same hand had just grasped a baseball bat and hit one out of the stadium. For Herb, being in the dugout with the Dodgers was a sanctuary.

After the game, Pee Wee Reese asked Herb if he'd like to hang out with the team in the dugout again some time. Herb nodded enthusiastically and said, "Yea. I mean, sure, thanks." Then Reese told him which gate to come to about an hour before the next home game, so that he could be escorted down to the dugout during batting practice.

Later that day, Herb went back home and played punch ball in the street in front of his apartment with a few of the guys in the neighborhood. Because there weren't enough kids to play all the positions, they played without a pitcher or a bat, and with plenty of "invisible" men. "You just punched the ball with your fist, then ran to first base—or got tagged out," Herb explained. Interestingly, he never told any of the kids that day about being in the Dodgers dugout. "I'm not sure why," he said. "Maybe I didn't want them to tease me, or think I was just making it up, or get jealous. And I didn't want them to think that I had just done something that they could not do. It was clearly something special. But it seemed otherworldly. As if it was not quite connected to the world I was living in."

Rubbing Shoulders with Heroes

At the next home game, they got Herb a seat right behind home plate. Enthused about the game, as it was about to begin, he started telling the woman sitting next to him about all the players, reciting each of their statistics, which he knew by heart. "She kept asking me questions, and I kept telling her all about the Dodgers," he said. "She bought me a hot dog and soda, and we spent the whole game talking. She asked me what my name was and I said, 'Herbie,' which is what they used to call me when I was a kid. And I asked her who she was and she said, 'Betty Grable'—the Hollywood actress who, in three years, would pose for an iconic bathing suit poster that would make her the number one pinup girl of World War II! As we got up to leave after the game, she kissed me goodbye on both cheeks. When I got home, my mother took one look at me and asked where I was in her thick Polish accent; so it sounded like, 'Ver vor you?' I told her, 'At Ebbets Field.' And she said, 'That's where you got the lipstick on your cheeks?' Then I just started laughing and told her that Betty Grable kissed me. 'Yeah, yeah, yeah, Betty Grable. And I suppose she's going to marry you tomorrow, right?'"

A few weeks later, Red Barber had Herb on his radio show called "My Favorite Kid." "It was fun, just for a few minutes," Herb recalled. "We talked about the last game, each of us exchanging impressions about the players and statistics about the team that we knew by heart."

Barber is considered by most sports announcers to be one of the ultimate role models. "I've heard tapes of Red Barber in the 1930s and '40s," Bob Costas told the *Los Angeles Times*, "where he tells you there's a line single to left-center and he tells you how many times it bounced before the center fielder picked it up. You needed that then. Today, even the very good announcers will very rarely describe a guy's stance or the peculiarities of a guy's windup, because they've been subconsciously influenced by television even though they're on the radio."

Herb's ability to paint a verbal picture certainly comes from listening very closely. When I was at his house once for a Super Bowl party, he had the television on, as well as the radio. When I asked him why, he said, "Close your eyes and just listen to the television. Then try to tell me what is happening." After a minute or two, it was clear that I couldn't describe the game to him. "Sports announcers on television assume you just saw the play, so they don't describe it to you. Instead, they'll fill the time with comments and statistics about the team or a player. The best radio announcers, however, not only tell you what is happening, but they paint a picture, so you get an appreciation for the story they are telling. That's why their voices are so important, and, at its best, their work often rises to the level of great art."

I can't help thinking that Herb may be hearing the same things we are all hearing, but paying a different kind of attention. It is as though the volume is turned up on each and every sound for him— because his hearing has to compensate for what he is not able to see. As a result, he often hears subtle cues that the rest of us might miss. It is interesting to consider that since he has to depend so much upon his hearing, Herb might actually be hearing better than the rest of us. This begs some questions: How can you, as a leader, hear more? Are you accurately hearing messages people are trying to tell you? What might you not be hearing? Are you open to hearing everything you need to? Sometimes, as leaders, we can inadvertently send the message that we are too busy to be bothered hearing certain things. Are you hearing what is important from everyone in your organization? Are you listening closely enough to your customers? Are sending the message that you are open to hearing about what might be going wrong, as well as what is going well? Are you taking the time you need to truly listen?

We'll return to the Dodgers, as they set the tone for Herb's childhood, fighting with everything they had, always coming close but not quite close enough, promising to come back again next year, finally winning a world series, then, unforgivably, leaving Brooklyn.

For now, however, just consider Herb as a kid growing up in that insular borough in the shadow of Manhattan. He would talk with his friends and his parents about what the Dodgers had to do to win next year. But then, he would also talk with the team's captain and short-stop, as well as the radio broadcaster who called play-by-plays for the team.

It is no wonder that the team's "wait till next year" spirit infused him. In many ways, the ability to rub shoulders at an early age with his sports heroes gave Herb the confidence to share his ideas and speak up for his beliefs. It was a world where heroes lived on the same street, or around the corner. They were approachable, grew up in the neighbor-hood, and were thrilled to be asked for their autograph.

That is amazing to consider: growing up in the same neighborhood as your heroes. Teenagers today may feel a certain connection with their sports or music heroes when they send a tweet or post a message on Facebook. They can dream of being invited backstage by Beyoncé to one of her concerts and then, after the concert, being kissed by her and asked if they'd like to go to a party with her. The truth, though, is that their heroes live in completely separate worlds, as if on Mount Olympus, so any possible connection with them is purely electronic. Herb was able to commiserate with his sports heroes about a missed opportunity or a lousy call by an umpire during a game earlier that day. And he cheered with them whenever they won. His heroes were like anyone else in the neighborhood, just a whole lot better at baseball. So there was an underlying message that Herb's dreams, like those of his heroes, could become real.

Seeing a Top Team in Action

Team sports certainly teach young children essential values—about cooperating, connecting, having a sense of camaraderie, knowing the importance of practicing, giving it your all, being part of a team, knowing how to win, knowing how to lose, having a positive attitude either way, and, ultimately, belonging to something bigger than yourself.

For Herb to have been able to experience such teamwork at the highest level undoubtedly instilled in him a deep sense of belonging and of confidence.

On the one hand, it is easy to see that being in the dugout with the Dodgers filled him with a sense that anything was possible. He had been taken under the wing of his heroes, accepted as part of the tribe. On the other hand, however, he didn't want to tell his friends because he thought he'd be ostracized. That's an interesting dilemma to carry into adulthood.

How has it affected him? How does he carry that experience with him now?

"In one sense, I am no longer awestruck by anyone. I see us all as equal in some ways, and special in other ways. We all are unique, and we all are similar. We all are different, and we all are alike. We can all be heroes and human, at the same time. I still have role models, people I respect and look up to. But I don't see them as being on a pedestal. I was certainly very pleased to meet President Obama and President Carter at different times. And I love that Vice President Joe Biden told me, 'What do you mean Mr. Vice President? To you, I'm *Joe*.' Still, whether they are royalty or presidents of countries, they are real people, with real talents, as well as real problems," Herb reflected. "So, I'm certainly not afraid to talk with anyone. We all have interesting stories. I'm just trying to make those connections."

Having been in the dugout with his heroes from his ultimate childhood dream team, Herb says, "I've experienced what can be at its very best. I've been with a team that showed what was possible. They connected with each other. They were there for each other. Pee Wee Reese put his arm around Jackie Robinson while a crowd shouted racial slurs, just to show everyone what he and they were all made of." He reflected, then added, "So now, I can sense when a team is working together and when there is conflict. I can feel it deep inside. I can sense that whenever we are with one of our clients. Ultimately I am drawn toward teams that 'get it.' And when teams are not in it together, I find it intolerable."

Psychological Insights—Confidence

"Confidence is the bridge connecting expectations with performance," according to Rosabeth Moss Kanter, a professor at the Harvard Business School and the former editor of the *Harvard Business Review*. In her book *Confidence*, she noted that individuals with confidence view a loss as a "crossroads, not a cliff." Confident individuals make mistakes and encounter troubles all the time, without falling off the edge. Then, when they have winning streaks, their confidence grows and helps propel a tradition of success.

Confidence is not an absolute, though. It has to do with degrees and situations. It is not an either/or. Nor is it always there. Herb agrees that confidence is not a personality quality. "Rather, it is a combination of factors that lead us to believe that we are confident in a particular situation; and people around us feel confident that we are confident," he says. In some ways, it is an experience that has to be mirrored. When we feel more confident, it is reflected in others, who, in turn, reflect that feeling of confidence back to us.

One of the most straightforward ways to increase our own confidence is to become more competent in what we are pursuing. Then, as we become more competent, our confidence rises. Ultimately, when we feel confident in someone, we are recognizing that they are competent, and *credible*.

"Still, it is important to recognize that there can be a chasm between *feeling* truly confident and *acting* confidently," Herb adds.

People who are *perceived* as being confident can convey to themselves and others that things will work; that the course they are on will succeed; that, together, they can change the tide. In this way, leaders who are confident that they can make things happen help to make things happen. Their confidence becomes a driving force, and it is mirrored by others, leading to increased confidence.

As Herb says, "Clearly, leaders need to be confident. But too much of a good thing can backfire. Overconfidence can actually lead to a leader's undoing. (This may sound contradictory, but stay with me for a minute.) A leader who is overconfident may create a shell around him- or herself so that others do not want to tell them something they absolutely need to hear, but that others fear might rub them the wrong way."

Confidence, as it turns out, is really a Goldilocks quality—it can't be too hot or too cold. It has to be just right.

"The goal of confidence," Herb adds, "is to anticipate success." The balancing act is for a leader to instill confidence in a mission and in others, while also being open to hearing counter-ideas.

Misguided or inappropriate levels of confidence can arise when leaders put themselves into bubbles. Then people around them do not want to pop their bubble. So they are just "yessing" them because they are afraid to say no.

"That is why a leader needs to be self-aware, so that he or she does not fall prey to the pitfalls of being overconfident," Herb says. For leaders, and potential leaders, the message is to be confident enough to make sure that you are not stopping yourself from hearing advice that is counter to what you are thinking or believing. What this takes is for a leader to be open enough to say, often and out loud, "Tell me what I am not thinking about that could possibly go wrong." Without encouraging such openness, if a leader is overconfident, those around him or her may feel it is not worth the psychological cost of expressing their doubts out loud. As a friend of mine says, the juice is not worth the squeeze.

How confident are leaders when facing "the Great Unknown"?

Allow me to share a quick story.

After the successful invasion of Normandy on what became known as D-Day, General Eisenhower gave a stirring speech in which he said, "The tide has turned. The free men of the world are marching together toward victory. I have full confidence in your courage, devotion to duty, and skill in battle."

However, the night before the invasion, Eisenhower woke at 3:30 in the morning, received an update on the weather, and gave the command for the attack to commence in the morning. Then he wrote a message that he fortunately never had to deliver to the American people and their allies around the world, in which he would have said, "Our landings . . . have failed. . . . If any blame or fault attaches to the attempt, it is mine alone." The general's leadership qualities are countless. What impresses me most about what he wrote, though, is that deep inside of him were enormous doubts. And he was willing to face them. Head-on. His confidence, courage, optimism, and hope were shrouded in doubt, fears, and worries. Anyone can be confident when success is guaranteed. Real confidence can only be tested in the face of adversity. That's when confidence shines through, creating new possibilities.

At the end of the day, confidence is an expectation of a positive outcome, while recognizing and accepting all of our doubts and fears. As Moss Kanter said, "Confidence is not a personality trait; it is an assessment of a situation that sparks motivation. If you have confidence, you're motivated to put in the effort, to invest the time and resources, and to persist in reaching the goal." Confidence can be the link between our expectations and performance. As Moss Kanter added, "It can be at the heart of why people with equal skill have different outcomes; and why teams sometimes perform above their talent level."

Our confidence, then, can become contagious.

Interestingly, the most lasting form of confidence is often not self-generated. Rather, our confidence can be nurtured by others—by our coaches, our parents, our partners, and our leaders. Then we, in turn, can return the favor to those with whom we surround ourselves.

Questions to Ask Yourself About Confidence

These questions are posed for you to consider as you create your own vision, tap into your personal strengths, and pursue your own leadership journey. Your answers to these questions will provide a starting point to consider the role that confidence plays in your approach to leadership. You are encouraged to consider these questions at different times, as your answers will undoubtedly evolve and change as your leadership journey unfolds.

1. Does the town or city where you are from give you strength—or a sense of meaning and purpose?
2. Is where you are from part of your personal leadership story?
3. When do you feel most confident?
4. When do you doubt yourself the most?
5. Are you comfortable with your doubt? Does it cause you to stop in your tracks? Or does it make you want to act?
6. Can you imagine having a conversation with one of your heroes? Who would it be? What would your first question be? Your second? Would you feel awe? Or a sense of belonging?
7. What quality does your hero possess that you would like to have?
8. What qualities do you and your hero both possess? If you focused more on that strength, how might that change your belief in yourself?

Spots Before His Eyes

"I remember waking up, early in the morning, to the sound of a little old man walking by our apartment, pushing his cart, calling out, 'Buy cash clothes. Buy cash clothes.' He was letting everyone know that he would buy our old clothes if we needed some extra cash, and he would sell us some old clothes for a price we could afford, if we needed them."

Hmmm. He wouldn't say, "Buy clothes for cash"?

"No." Calling out, imitating the voice he heard as a child, Herb repeated, "It was 'Buy cash clothes.' I guess that's why I remember it. And his voice was so distinct," Herb said. "I can still hear it in my sleep," like a faint reminder of what was.

"Then the milkman would come by a few times a week to deliver a couple of quarts of milk in glass bottles and take the old ones back,"

Herb said. "And the iceman would *cometh*, as Eugene O'Neill said, to bring huge blocks of ice, since we had no refrigerator."

Where would the ice go?

"In the bottom, in the lower part of what we called the *icebox*. The ice would be cut to fit inside the box. So you wouldn't buy groceries for a week, like people do today. You'd just buy for a day or so. Anything you bought had to be able to stay fresh on ice, before it melted," he said, smiling at the recollection. "In fact, years later when we actually got a refrigerator, we still called it the icebox."

So you would be wakened either by the guy selling clothes, or the milkman or the iceman?

"Yeah, but I was always an early riser, anyway." He paused, then said, "You know, Brooklyn is bigger than you think. If it was a city by itself, it would be the country's fourth largest city. New York is the first, but it needs Brooklyn to be that."

So Brooklyn would be the country's fourth largest city, and the largest neighborhood. "That's interesting, Herb," I said. "That you would even think of severing Brooklyn from Manhattan shows that there is a rivalry. Can you explain the rivalry for those of us who did not grow up in either place?"

"We hated the Giants more than the Yankees. I mean we hated the Yankees, but the Giants were in the same league. So we could beat the Giants 22 times during the season and never even play the Yankees unless we got them in the World Series," he said, trying to explain the rivalry. "Of course, they play each other now. But back then, no one played interleague games."

Both the Giants and the Yankees were from Manhattan, across one of the bridges from Brooklyn. But they represented another world. For Herb, this rivalry meant he, like everyone else from Brooklyn, was a runner-up, perpetually coming in just behind the winner, but believing they had a plan for reprisal. That "wait till next year" spirit of the Dodgers became part of Herb's psyche. It was more than just background music. This feeling infused how he played as a kid and how he would come to work as an adult. "Waiting," he added, "was not about being patient. It meant preparing and believing that next year would be ours."

"Look, the Dodgers were, I mean, we used to call ourselves The Bums. You didn't get dressed up to go to a Dodgers game. And the players were one of us. We were all bums."

You were all bums?

"We were all bums. And there was a certain pride in that," he paused, then added, "Manhattan was a place to go. You'd go there for the theater or the nightclubs. You'd go out to Manhattan and get dressed up. But it wasn't where we lived. Or where you wanted to live," he said, "Not if you were from Brooklyn."

When Herb was nine years old, around the same time the Dodgers just barely lost another close game, he became very ill from an infected mastoid, which is the cranial bone behind the ear. "I was burning up with fever, so my parents had to get me to the hospital for an operation right away. My condition was quite serious," he says. "My parents were told that it was likely that I would lose my hearing, and that there was a very real possibility that I might not make it through the operation." As it turned out, he had to have a double mastoid operation. *"I never learned how to do anything halfway," he says, smiling.*

Then he pauses, adding, "Now, you also have to understand that my parents were already in excruciating emotional pain at that time. Just a few days before I was rushed to the hospital, my 13-month-old baby sister, Rosalind, died from a strep throat. I can't imagine what they were going through. And, as fate would have it, penicillin was introduced a few years later and could have cured both my sister's strep throat and my mastoid infection."

However, at the time, he says, he felt extremely guilty for taking his parent's attention away from his sister's death. "I didn't want them to have to deal with another problem, and the last thing I wanted in the world was for that problem to be me," he says, shaking his head. He pauses, then says, "All I could think was, 'Why her?'" He pauses again, then adds, "Why not me?" He resolved that he must have been saved for some reason.

While Herb's operation was successful, he left the hospital feeling very frail. "I just felt too weak to do anything," he says. "I had lost a lot of weight, and the doctors also said that I was extremely susceptible to infection.

"To build up my strength and breathe in some fresh air," Herb said, "my parents took me down the shore, then to the Pinelands in New Jersey, where I remember riding in a horse and buggy. But, as I was feeling stronger, I also started to see spots in front of my eyes. I never told my parents about it; I'd just rub my eyes and the spots would go away."

But the spots kept reappearing.

As it turned out, he says, "A rare strand of virus hit my eyes, but we didn't know it at the time." As a result, over the course of that year, as Herb grew stronger, his vision slowly faded.

The spots were getting bigger and bigger. And they stopped going away.

His sister Linda, who is eight years younger than Herb, remembers him holding books so close that he would completely cover his face, trying to read the words. "Then, one day, I was reading a book to my dad from the Don Sturdy series of adventure stories, and my father couldn't help but notice that I was holding the book upside down."

You cannot help but wonder what was going through Herb's mind at that time.

"It was very confusing. It just wasn't making sense anymore. There were all these black marks and dots on the white paper, but I didn't know what they meant. I could only remember what we read out loud in class. I was just repeating what I had memorized."

So his parents rushed Herb to the doctor, where all doubt about what was happening was removed. "I can remember him saying, 'Your son is going blind. There is nothing we can do,'" Herb said. "While, to me, it seemed to happen in an instant, I know it was a slow process, very gradual. It probably occurred over the course of a year. There wasn't any one crashing moment when I thought, 'Oh, my God, I'm blind.' And I don't remember crying or asking, 'Why me?' or 'What am I going to do?' I just kept adjusting. As the black dots got bigger and started to take over, I just kept trying to look closer and closer at things. And, honest to God, I didn't realize, except for the black dots, that anything was wrong. It didn't really hit me until one of the follow-up doctor visits when I heard him say, 'Your son is blind.'"

What Is It Like for Him to Be Blind?

If you don't mind my asking, Herb, can you see anything at all?

"Right now, I can make out just a bit of light. Today is a very sunny day. It is very bright, and I can see some light. I know the sun is over there," he said, pointing upward and somewhat to the west.

Light and shadows, however, are about it.

"I don't see any color," he continues, "just bright and dark areas. I can't see shapes. Not really. I can sense that you are right there. But it is just because you are blocking the light. You are an indistinguishable shape."

How Much of Our Senses Do We Really Use?

Does the loss of one of your senses improve your other senses?

"I can't tell you for sure. I don't have anything to compare it to," Herb said.

In experimental studies, it has been shown that people who are blind often outperform sighted individuals when they are requested to focus their attention on one sensory modality—such as sound, taste, smell, or temperature.

As William James so artfully said, "Compared to what we ought to be, we are only half awake." In other words, many of us use only a small part of our physical and mental resources. James concluded that we all possess "powers of various sorts" that we "habitually [fail] to use."

How else can one explain Herb's uncanny awareness of time, distance, and direction? He seems to have a built-in compass and clock. He has a memory for phone numbers like a Rolodex file and can get you from here to there much faster than a GPS.

A while back, I was driving with Herb from the airport into downtown Miami to speak at a convention. Herb had stayed at the hotel before, and we were on in a little over an hour, so he said, "Just head south on A1A." "How far is it?" I asked. He smiled and said, "Don't worry, I'll tell you when to make a turn. Let's just review what we're going to do when we get there." Knowing how to take a hint, I focused with him on the last-minute details of our presentation. Then he said, "Where are we now?" I looked around and said, "At a light, across the street from a Texaco station." He said, "No, I mean, what street are we crossing?" I told him, and he said, "Fine. We're only about a half-mile away. The hotel will be on your right."

I asked him, "How in the world did you know exactly where we were?" He replied, "It's not that I was thinking about it all that intensely. It's all just peripheral. I'm aware of the same things you are, but in a different way. While both of us were involved in the conversation, you were probably also looking at the scenery for landmarks or whatever. Right? You're not concentrating on it. It's just part of the background. I'm more aware of the road, the turns, and our speed because my energy and attention are not wasted taking in the scenery."

Directions are more than just getting from point A to point B for Herb. "I've got to know where I am," he said. "I need to know if we are on the right track. Are we getting lost? Are we okay? I have to know because most people don't have a clear sense of where they are or where they are going. Maybe it's a control thing on my part. But somebody's got to know where we are going and what is happening. And I feel better if it's me."

I pointed out to him that this sounded a lot like his management style.

"I hadn't thought of it that way, but I think you're right." He said, "I don't want to have to tell people what to do all the time. I just want to know what's going on and that we're moving in the right direction. Tell me what's happening. If it's good, that's great. I always love to hear positive things. If it's bad, let me know, so we can fix it. *But I can't know whether we're on track or have a problem until I know where we're headed and what the plan is for getting there.*"

As a leader, Herb's message is about constantly connecting. You want to keep connecting with ideas and with people. Ultimately, there is no substitute for connecting in real and meaningful ways with everyone on your team. Sure, you need to have regular team meetings, as well as individual meetings with everyone intermittently. Equally important, though, is being accessible in very informal ways. When Ed Koch was the popular mayor of New York, he used to ride the subway system and stand on street corners greeting those passing by with his slogan, "How 'm I doin'?" While your style may be very different from the mayor's, the straightforward openness of his question is worth keeping in mind. The point is to welcome everyone you encounter in a way that allows them to feel comfortable opening up to you. Some people may prefer to just tell you positive things, while others will be willing to let you know concerns that are on their mind. To get to the heart of the matter, you might ask a variation on the mayor's question, such as, "Tell me about something that is going incredibly well here." Then follow it with, "And how could we make one thing better?" The style and manner in which you ask the questions, of course, need to be your own. What is most important is to be open, encouraging, and inviting. That will keep your connections strong, as you take in myriad perspectives. You are looking for insights and perceptions that you would otherwise miss. Then, the more information you can filter through, the more clearly you'll see your way to the future.

As Herb adds, "It's all about knowing directions. It's about knowing where you've been and where you're going."

An Experiment

What is it like not to be able to see?

Ask someone you trust implicitly to blindfold you and walk around with your arm in his or hers for five minutes That's all. Just five minutes.

You're going to find out just how long five minutes can last.

Afterward, write down what the experience felt like. How safe did you feel at first? Did you feel safer as time passed? How fast did you feel you were going? At what point did you want to just stop and open your eyes? What did you learn about trust? Were you completely trusting the person you were walking with? Were you trusting yourself? Did you learn anything about trusting your own instincts?

Psychological Insights—Trust

Yor realize just how important trust is when you walk with someone who is blind. When a blind person is holding onto your arm, that person must trust you to look out for him or her. You are the person's guide. Where's the wall? Is there a curb? Are you sure you're paying close enough attention, watching out for both of you?

I was with Herb and his friend, venture capitalist Gordon Gund, who lost his sight at the age of thirty-one, when they engaged in an interesting conversation about trust. They both admitted that it took a long time for each of them to allow other people to help them. But as they learned to let down their guard, they realized that acceptance, and the subsequent trust, helped them develop deeper relationships.

After Gordon became blind, he decided he didn't want to give up downhill skiing. Since 1965, he's been skiing with the same instructor. "While we're skiing, he's about five feet behind me, and he'll say 'Go' every few seconds just so we're in touch. If I'm getting a little off, he'll just say, 'Hold right' or 'hold left.' It's an incredible sense of freedom. I can move *fast*, unimpeded. And I can feel the mountain," Gordon's smile kept growing as he reflected. "Without sight, you develop a keener sense of touch and feel. You have to rely on your other senses. And you also need to have more trust—in others and in yourself."

While admiring Gordon's courage, though freely admitting that downhill skiing is the furthest thing from his mind (and he is absolutely content keeping it that way), Herb agreed that trust becomes a more immediate issue when you are blind. "Even just walking with someone for the first time, whether in a business or personal situation, our relationship becomes closer, faster than most people are used to. Because I need to depend upon them, there is a level of comfortableness and trust that has to be shown immediately."

Trust is at the heart of any relationship that is working. Can you depend on someone? If you were in a tough spot, would that person be there for you? You might trust someone's ability, but do you trust that that person would keep your confidence? That he or she would have your back, no matter what?

The depth of our relationships, whether personal or professional, all come down to questions about trust. Do we trust each other? Do you trust me? Do I believe in you? Are we there for each other? Do I feel that you will come through for me? Do you believe I have your back? And if any of these questions can be answered with a "no," then trust is probably not there.

You can tell when there is trust. It has to do with how much distance there is (or is not) between you and someone else. For leaders, the lesson is that in our personal and professional relationships, we can feel one of two things: trust or distance. Trust is an either-or. It can't be faked. At the end of the day, trust is at the heart of who we are—and at the center of our deepest connections.

Questions to Ask Yourself About Trust

These questions are posed for you to consider as you create your own vision, tap into your personal strengths, and pursue your own leadership journey. Your answers to these questions will provide insights into how trust plays into your approach to leadership. You are encouraged to consider these questions at different times, as your answers will undoubtedly evolve and change as your leadership journey unfolds.

1. Whom do you trust?
2. Who trusts you?
3. If you were in a tough spot, would that person be there for you?
4. If that person said he or she needed to talk, would you drop what you were doing and be there?
5. Do you believe that trust and doubt are opposites?
6. When has your trust ever been broken?
7. Were you able to rebuild it?

Learning What to Accept and What to Fight For

Throughout the interminably long year when Herb lost his sight, he and his parents alternately challenged and accepted what had happened. Herb started taking Braille lessons right away. "But I found reading Braille to be tedious. For me, memorizing was a lot easier," Herb recalls. In fact, he claims to have never taken a note in all his school days—from elementary school to getting his Ph.D.

Meanwhile, his intensity, impatience, and anger merged to defy a well-meaning but inept educational system that wanted to send him away to a special school for the blind. His parents were told that there were three distant schools he could attend, but they would have nothing to do with them. They refused to allow their young son to be sent away to school. He had just lost his sight, and they didn't want him to lose touch with his family and friends. They were determined to make sure he lived at home. But more important, they wanted Herb to attend a regular school with kids in the neighborhood. They didn't want him to be segregated because of his blindness, and they clearly understood that their son felt the same way because he told them, in no uncertain terms, "If you let them send me away, I'll break every window in the building."

During that time, Herb remembers, his parents continued to take him to the mountains in upstate New York and to the Pine Barrens in New Jersey to make sure he was getting the fresh air the doctors told them he needed. Finally, the stalemate was broken when a representative from the board of education came to their apartment with news that a school in Brooklyn, P.S. 93, had a Braille class Herb could attend.

Looking back on that year, Herb views his parents' strong stance as a turning point. "If they had caved in and sent me away to a school for the blind," he said, "I have no doubt, particularly back then, that my options would have been very limited and my life would have been completely different."

This is a lesson that Herb still ponders, and never takes for granted. There are certain times when compromising makes absolute sense. Then there are other times when compromising is not an option, when we need to stand our ground. How can we know, when we are in the midst of a situation, when to find common ground and when to stand our ground? While diplomacy is often what is needed to ease difficult situations, if, as a leader, you find yourself compromising too much, then you have to ask yourself if you are really leading. Leading starts with being clear about what you are willing to accept and what you need to fight for.

Another lesson from this time that Herb still carries with him is his father saying that he had to be "just a little better." Herb explains, "That didn't mean I had to be better than anyone else," he says. "I understood that he meant that I had to be as good as I possibly could, to keep pushing, to keep trying, to keep stretching—because I was going to come across some people who might have their own prejudices about what blind people could and could not do. So I needed to be 'just a little better' to show them that I could surpass their expectations." And Herb carried that message about continually improving with him, getting a little better at whatever he was (and is) doing on his own journey. That message—of persistently striving, never quite being completely satisfied—is still an essential part of how Herb describes himself today.

Making Everyone Feel Welcome

Herb and I went back to 761 St. Marks Avenue, the six-story brownstone apartment building that he and his family called home so long ago, then walked the half-dozen blocks to P.S. 93, his elementary school. That was where, luckily, as it turned out for Herb, his homeroom teacher Ms. Gertrude Ruhman was, as he describes, a godsend, she would start the day by making sure that Herb and the other students in her room were ready for the day. "She was absolutely wonderful," Herb gushes. "She was a great teacher who made me feel very much that I belonged there." She'd check to make sure that Herb and the other students had all their homework assignments complete, ask if they were struggling with any particular subject, help them with whatever they needed, and verify that they knew where their classes were for the day. Then at the end of the day, she would make sure that Herb and his classmates understood what they had to do for their homework assignments.

It was there, in third grade, that Herb learned Braille, though, as he says, "I didn't really have the patience for it. I can read Braille fine. It's just tedious. Whenever I could figure out how to learn something without reading it in Braille, that's what I would do. Because Braille just slowed things down too much for me."

Inside the school was a place where Herb felt secure. It was where his sharp listening skills and keen memory were given the opportunity to kick into high gear. He liked focusing intently as he listened to his teachers, making sure he was getting every nuance. Then, because of his uncanny recall, he was ready to raise his hand whenever a question was asked or give the right response on a test. "Oh, I loved school. I felt a sense of belonging and achieving there," he reflects. School was the place where Herb was in his zone, honing his hearing and his memory, which would give him two clear advantages for the rest of his life.

How can these early childhood experiences of Herb's relate to your leadership journey? As a leader, it is worth pausing from time to time, and thinking about the environment you are creating around you. Do others feel safe and secure around you? Do they feel that you are there for them? Do they feel that you encourage them to stretch their abilities and discover their real potential? At the end of the day, when people feel secure around us, they can surprise themselves and us as they tap into and expand their capabilities. Consider the environment you are creating. Be conscious about it. Those you surround yourself with will give it their all when they feel safe, secure, and part of something bigger than themselves. They are looking for you to set the tone. And that tone can make all the difference in the world.

Fighting Back

The only problem Herb had with school was getting there. PS 93 was just a few blocks away, so the distance was not a concern. However, he had to walk through Bedford-Stuyvesant, one of Brooklyn's toughest areas, and he would often get beat up along the way.

It is daunting to consider that Herb grew up in a neighborhood where someone would actually attack a blind kid.

Herb explains, "There were quite a few times when I was attacked, punched, and in some cases, really beaten up. That's why, to this day,

I need my right hand free. I needed to make sure that when the attacks came, I was ready"

To this day, whenever I walk with him, Herb always wants to link his left arm inside my right arm. It's just a pattern, and I never gave it much thought until one time when we were rushing through an airport and I went to tuck his other arm inside of mine. He went out of his way to switch positions. When I asked him why, he explained that even though the last fistfight he was in was as a kid, he still likes to walk with someone on his left so that his right hand is free to swing. "I can't remember the last time I had to slug anyone," he said, laughing slightly. "It's just a deep-seated preservation thing," he explains.

So what happened to this blind 11-year-old, walking to school, that would cause such haunting memories to this day?

From his former apartment at 761 St. Marks Avenue, we walk the six blocks to P.S. 93, tracing the route that Herb would take daily to get to his elementary school. When we cross Bergen Street, Herb says, "Now we are in Bedford-Stuyvesant. And somewhere between Bergen and Dean Street is where I would get beat up on my way to school." At that point, I can feel his arm tighten just a bit, as if preparing himself for a possible attack. All these years later, places where positive or negative things occurred can still hold a very specific energy for us.

Who would hit a blind kid on his way to school? The nearsighted kids? What was that about?

"I was an easy target. Don't you understand?"

"No," I said. "I really don't."

"Well, I didn't have to understand it," he says. "I just had to learn how to defend myself. And take a few punches and give a few, while I was at it."

How would it start?

"As soon as I heard, 'Hey, Boy,' I knew what would happen next. It was never so bad that I couldn't go to school. But after 'Hey, Boy,' I was about to get punched. So I'd get ready to try to throw a couple of punches back before they'd leave me and whichever friend was walking with me alone," he adds.

His sister Linda recalls that after Herb swung in self-defense and knocked down one of the gang members, he actually started coming to the apartment to see if he could walk Herb to school.

Herb and I then come to Pacific Street, where I tell him there is a Range Rover parked outside of someone's house.

"Really? Boy, this place *has* changed," he says.

Then we walk across Atlantic Avenue, where a train rumbles overhead.

"That would be the Long Island Railroad," Herb says loudly, so he can be heard over the sound of the passing train. He breathes in the memory, as if it were a faint scent, then he calls out, "The next block will be Herkimer, and that's where the school is."

As we walk under the tracks of the Long Island Railroad, with the thundering sounds echoing overhead, it is easy to imagine a chase scene being filmed there, with cars speeding after one another, weaving in and out.

Ten minutes after we start, we arrive at P.S. 93, a tall, imposing school that has just celebrated its 100th birthday and now houses over 300 students from pre-kindergarten through fifth grade, promising to "develop a positive sense of self-esteem, self-worth and purpose for each student who attends."

As we walk inside the school, Herb says "I have very fond feelings about this school. I got a great education here, a great start." Inside of that school is where his keen memory got a steady workout as he would listen and memorize every word his teachers said. That training, keenly developing his memory, would become his ace in the hole.

———

After school let out that summer, Herb's parents sent him for a month to a camp for blind and visually impaired children that had just opened in northeastern Vermont on a lake surrounded by 220 wooded acres. There was camping, canoeing, swimming, hiking and nature study. While it sounds idyllic, ironically, Herb found himself getting beat up by anti-Semitic bullies who were several years older. "On my way to the infirmary each day," Herb says, "these bigots would jump me from behind and start pummeling me. At first, I didn't know what was happening. Then I started to expect it and was ready to swing back. But it got to be too much."

In the middle of one night, Herb snuck out of his cabin and walked to the camp's mess hall, where he broke in and, with a pocket full of coins, called his parents from a pay phone. "They came," he says, "which they could ill afford to do. But the counselors convinced my parents that I was just homesick, and that staying would be the best thing for me." For the next few weeks, Herb was constantly attacked by those bullies who would curse and call him "a dirty Jew-bastard" as they hit him. Finally, the last day, Herb says, he just could not take it anymore and jumped on the leader of the group and started swinging with everything he had.

When he got home, Herb says he showed his parents his bruises. "But they could only half-believe it," he said. "I don't think they wanted to believe that they had sent me someplace so nice that could turn out so bad. They felt they were doing the best thing in the world for me. Emotionally, I don't think they could quite accept what really happened. So, we just turned the page on that chapter, and never talked about it again. But, at least for myself, I knew that I had caused as much harm to the leader of that gang of bigots as he had caused to me. And I slept better for it."

The word they use in Brooklyn is *moxie*. It's more than courage. It comes with an I'll-show-you attitude. "I never started a fist fight. But I had enough moxie to stand up for myself if I was attacked, and, at least, try to get a good slug in." Pausing, he adds, *"At the very least,*

I've learned to defend myself, and to fight for what I believe, whatever the odds."

As we will see later, this theme of having to fight for what he believes in has played itself out throughout Herb's life. Nothing is given to him, he learned. Anything important has to be fought for—including his principles. While, as time goes by, the fighting becomes less physical, it is still about taking on an opponent and standing up for what he believes in. It cannot help but make you wonder: *What are you willing to fight for?*

Could We Finally Get a Win?

So while this recreational camp seemed more like a boxing camp, Herb's summer was not a complete washout. As that summer of 1941 led into the fall, it looked like the Dodgers might actually have a World Series championship team. They were in their zone. Everything was clicking for them. Dolph Camilli had 34 home runs. Pete Reiser led the league in batting average. They had Hall of Famers everywhere you looked. They scored 800 tines that season. There seemed to be no stopping them. And Herb got to spend several games back in the dugout.

The Dodgers beat the St. Louis Cardinals to win the pennant, and they could taste what it would be like to beat their archrivals the New York Yankees in the World Series. It became known as the first Subway Series because it was played between two New York City teams.

Through Herb's hearty voice and impeccable memory, we hear: "Okay. So here's what the World Series Brooklyn Dodgers team looked like. Are you ready?"

I'm all set.

"We've got Dolph Camilli at first base. Second base, Billy Herman. Shortstop, my favorite, Pee Wee Reese."

These are great names: Dolph and Pee Wee.

"They are. Then we've got Cookie Lavagetto at third. In left field, we've got Joe Medwick. Center field is Pete Reiser. Right field, Dixie Walker."

You're sounding just like Red Barber.

"Thanks. The catcher is Mickey Owen. And, of course, pitching we've got Whitlow Wyatt, Kirby Higbe, Fat Freddie Fitzsimmons, and the famous relief pitcher Hugh Casey."

Herb paused, then said, "I'm going to take you back to Ebbets Field on Sunday, October fifth, to the game where the World Series slipped out of our hands"

Were you there?

"Not for that one."

Still, that kind of hurt doesn't go away.

"It doesn't. Casey struck out Henrich, which would have ended the game. That was game four of the series, and it would have been tied two games apiece. With the momentum in our favor. But, Mickey Owen somehow couldn't catch Casey's sharply breaking curveball. It hit off his glove, and by the time he got it Henrich had made it to first—which is what a batter's allowed to do when a catcher misses a ball—even if it is on a strikeout pitch. After that, all hell broke lose. Everything changed, inside out. We felt the World Series slip through our hands, just like that ball had slipped through Mickey Owen's glove. There didn't seem to be anything we could do at that point. The next thing you know Joe DiMaggio hit a single, and the Yankees got into a rally that took them from losing to winning 7 to 4. And, with it, they changed the tide of the World Series. The tide was no longer on our side."

Sometimes, pain and hope can ride alongside of each other. It's hard to fathom. Impossible to explain. Feeling the hurt and the pride at the same time. "We had a shot at it. It was ours. We were leading. Then it was over," Herb said. "The World Series was in our hands, then it disappeared. Poof. In one fleeting moment, everything changed. It was in, then out, then over. All over. And there was nothing that could be done," as Herb says, "but to know that there will always be next year."

How do your losses—whether personal or professional—affect you? Do you carry them with you? Do they drive you to try again? Can you remember each and every one of them? Or do you shrug them off? What we learn from life's necessary losses has a lot to do with defining who we are—and who we will become.

Psychological Insights—Resilience

Where does self-esteem come from? How can you develop it? Leadership is about knowing what to stand for—and against.

While it is not a formula, leadership starts with being able to convey confidence, having a clear perspective and asserting it, communicating with a direct style, having an inner need to bring others around to your point of view—and getting back up when you've been knocked down.

How do you handle rejection, defeat, or just the slings and arrows that life may shoot your way?

"Essentially," Herb says, "individuals with a healthy, intact ego have a positive picture of themselves. This is the quality that can enable them to brush themselves off when they get knocked down and carry on with even more determination."

When all is said and done, resilience has a lot to do with defining who you are.

"Everyone, no matter how successful, will fail, be rejected, and face personal defeats," Herb adds.

The question is: How do you deal with those situations?

Leading has a great deal to do with how you handle adversity. Do you shut down? Or open up? Do you put your head down and just keep doing what you were doing before? A little faster, a little harder? Or do you look around for a new path?

The difference has to do with how you will lead—and who you will become in the process.

People with resilience—and it is virtually impossible to lead without it—have an unusual way of viewing rejection. They are able to learn from negative experiences and, in some cases, turn them into defining moments.

How does that happen?

First, we have to recognize that most of us, when we are rejected, have enough common sense to say, "Well, that wasn't a whole lot of fun. I'm certainly not going to do that again."

We don't go out of our way to look for negative experiences.

But people with resilience demonstrate a unique approach toward dealing with situations that don't go their way. Herb says, "They feel the sting of being set back. They may even dwell on it, feel slightly diminished, and tend to be a little self-critical. But then they muster their determination, shake off any negative feelings, and learn what they need to do to carry on. It's like a voice in the back of their heads that says, 'I'll show you,' and then pushes them forward."

Essentially, individuals who have the talent and ambition to lead, yet who receive signals, whether subtle or overt, that others think they will not make the grade, use their resilience to fuel their ambition.

It's all a matter of whether we learn from our mistakes or repeat them. Do we internalize the rejections and accept them, or challenge them and shake them off?

Leading has much to do with how you overcome negative experiences. It is knowing that rejection is all just part of the game. Nothing personal.

"Individuals with resilience feel just as bad as anyone would when they encounter failure," Herb notes, "but they react to that failure much as someone who is hungry does to missing a meal: They are that much hungrier for the next opportunity."

The failure, though disappointing, does not destroy their positive view of themselves. "The failure is not personalized but rather creates a disappointment—a lack of fulfillment—that the next opportunity will correct," he adds.

On the other hand, people who do not have sufficient resilience—if they do not have enough positive feelings about themselves—will take the rejection to heart. They will therefore be very hesitant to seek another situation that could incur yet another rejection because the pain would be too much to bear.

"Without enough resilience, therefore, leading would be like trying to defy gravity," Herb says.

It is important to note, however, that many people confuse resilience with toughness. Toughness is an aspect of resilience, certainly. Being tough can be an advantage in certain circumstances. But only to a certain point. This is so because toughness also can create an armor that deflects emotion. And it can cut us off from many of the resources we need to bounce back. Most important, it can cut us off from the people around us.

Resilience, by contrast, is very different. Resilience is not about deflecting challenges. Resilience is about absorbing those challenges and rebounding even stronger than before.

People with resilience actually want to change the future and in the process alter the effects that the past had on them. When things do not go their way, after catching their breath, they want to get back in the game. The negative experience propels them. They want to fight it. They want it gone. Out of their memories. It's as if their minds are like tape recorders—and they want to tape over what didn't work out, replacing it with a successful outcome.

A scholar, organizational consultant, and author Warren Bennis wrote, "The skills required to conquer adversity and emerge even stronger and more committed than ever are the same ones that make for extraordinary leaders." Through interviewing and studying leaders, he has found that they were all able to point to "intense, often traumatic experiences that had transformed them and had become the sources of their distinctive leadership abilities." He calls these "crucible experiences," noting that such trials caused the leaders to enter a state of deep self-reflection, questioning who they were and what mattered most to them. Invariably, he says, these leaders emerged from these experiences "stronger and more sure of themselves and their purpose—changed in some fundamental way."

How you handle rejection as a leader, ultimately, has to do with how you will lead and who you will become.

Questions to Ask Yourself About Resilience

These questions are posed for you to consider as you create your own vision, tap into your personal strengths, and pursue your own leadership journey. Your answers to these questions will help you understand how your resilience will come into play as a leader. You are encouraged to consider these questions at different times, as your answers will undoubtedly evolve and change as your leadership journey unfolds.

1. What can you accept?
2. What can you *not* accept?
3. Are you clear about what you will fight for?
4. What is the hardest thing you've had to overcome? What did you learn about yourself from that experience? Which details still linger with you from that experience?
5. What has been your biggest mistake? What did you learn about yourself from it?
6. When something goes wrong, how long does it take for you to get over it? What part of that negative experience do you carry with you?
7. How do you help others when they are dealing with rejection, failure, or just the slings and arrows that life has a tendency to shoot our way?
8. What is your next big challenge? Are you ready for it?
9. What childhood lessons do you still carry with you? How do they form your beliefs about yourself? Are those beliefs still accurate?

Getting from Here to There

Floating in a lake in upstate New York, Herb smiled up at the warm sun, then took a deep breath and dove down as far as he could. Touching the bottom, he pushed off and came up, gasping for air. The 12-year old would spend this and his next three summers at this Boy Scout camp, connecting with kids from all across the state, competing, cooperating, and just having fun. This was such a completely different experience from the first camp he had gone to, where he was mercilessly beat up by anti-Semitic bullies. At first, Herb said, he had nightmares about going to another camp. His scoutmaster, though, encouraged him to let those tears go.

"It's hard to explain what being accepted into the Boy Scouts meant to me," Herb says. "Initially, I was told that I could join a Boy Scout troop in the upper Bronx, which was exclusively for blind kids.

But there was no way my parents could get me there in time for the meetings after school."

"Finally, Lionel Goldman, the scoutmaster of Troop 271 [which met at his elementary school], said he'd take a chance on me. And he became one of my mentors," Herb adds. It was there that Herb felt, as he says, "accepted, challenged, and just one of the kids."

For Herb, once again, like his experience of going to school, getting accepted into the Boy Scouts took the intervention of someone who was willing to stick his neck out and give this young blind boy a shot at being just a normal, everyday kid.

By bending the rules and allowing a blind boy into his troop, Herb said, Lionel gave him the chance to make new friends and do things he never would have otherwise, including spending four summers at camp. "Lionel was comfortable with my being blind. He didn't view it as something that should hold me back. I'm eternally grateful to him for that," Herb says.

Under Lionel's tutelage, Herb went on to become a patrol leader, an assistant scoutmaster, and a Life Scout. But simply being "one of the guys" was what mattered most to Herb at that time. "It was so much fun," he says. "We were all good at different things. We all had a shot of standing out in one way or another. And we worked together, in teams. One of my specialties happened to be knot tying. I could tie all nine knots more accurately and faster than anyone else whenever we had team competitions, whether it was a square knot, the sheepshank, the bowline, or two half hitches, which you use for horses."

Not bad for a city kid.

His favorite part of being a Boy Scout was summer camp at Ten Mile River, in New York's Catskills, just outside of Narrowsburg. "To get there, you'd take the Erie Railroad and get off at Port Jarvis station," Herb explained. There he could swim, canoe, sing songs around a campfire, and go hiking in the hills along the Delaware River.

Herb says, "I still remember most of those camp songs. Would you like to hear one now?"

Let's hold off on that for just a little bit.

When he was a senior in high school, Herb was just two merit badges shy of being an Eagle Scout (the highest rank attainable in the Boy Scout program). But he had little hope of getting those badges. The one was in bird study, and the other was in lifesaving. "I happen to be a strong swimmer," he said, "but I couldn't get the merit badge for lifesaving because you had to dive down to the bottom of a lake, find a 20-pound ball, bring it up, and swim to shore with it. Of course, since I couldn't see, there was no way that I could find the ball. Then when it came to the bird study, I was able to remember all of the colors of the birds and I could imitate some of their sounds, but I couldn't point them out in the sky, since I couldn't see them." While the Scout Master was supportive of Herb in every way possible, he could not completely bend the rules to allow Herb to become an Eagle Scout. That was until just 10 years ago when, in a special ceremony, the Boy Scouts named Herb an honorary Eagle Scout.

In Herb's life, Lionel Goldman arrived at just the right time. As we reflect on our own lives, it is interesting to think about a time when a mentor appeared for us. Have you ever heard the saying "When the student is ready, the teacher will appear"? Has that ever happened to you? Were you seeking a mentor? Were you searching for an answer? Were you open to a new experience? Do you see the world as creating unforeseen possibilities?

If you have not found a mentor, perhaps the question is: Are you ready?

In Greek mythology, when Odysseus went off to fight the Trojan War, he selected Mentor to advise his son in the legendary king's absence. Since then, the term "mentor" has been adapted as a term meaning someone who imparts wisdom to a less-experienced colleague.

In addition to providing sound advice and wisdom, mentors also share an abiding connection with their protégés. Often mentors and protégés connect on a very deep level with each other because they recognize or sense a part of themselves in each other. Particularly when we are in the midst of a challenging time, a mentor can provide the special connection we need, allowing our hearts to be felt and our thoughts to be heard.

A mentor may help you on your leadership journey by accompanying you for part of the way, preparing you for something you may not be ready for, listening and allowing you to come to your own conclusions, revealing how your thought patterns may be holding you back, and just believing in you.

That special connection with your mentor can also help you realize that you are not alone on your leadership journey—that you are connected to a long and noble past. That connection can help you persevere through times of uncertainty and prepare you to face the unknown with confidence.

Ultimately, a mentor will help you not just to find the right answers—but to ask the right questions.

If you have been fortunate enough to have a mentor, the next question is: Are you ready to return the favor? Are you ready to be a mentor to someone else? Have you opened yourself up to the possibility? And will you know when the student has found you?

————————

It is daunting to ponder the sheer determination it took for Herb just to get to school, let alone to excel there. Just consider: to get to Bushwick High School, he would walk, with his cane, to Utica Avenue, where he would catch a trolley that would take him to Gates Avenue. From there, he would catch a trolley that would take him to Irving Street. From there, it was a short walk to Bushwick High School, which took up an entire city block. "Getting there was a drag," he says. "Assuming all of the trolleys were on time, it would take a little over an hour each way. But all it would cost was a nickel, because once you bought a ticket, the route transfers were free all day."

When he got to school, Herb continued memorizing. He memorized his way through elementary, junior high, and senior high school. He memorized facts and figures that intrigued him, as well as information that bored him to tears. Rather than take notes and refer back to what he needed, Herb found it easier to listen intently to his teachers and turn his mind into a tape recorder. "I never cut class," he says, "because I needed to hear everything the teacher was saying. That's how I would learn. I remember some kids would ask me how I was doing it, as if there was some trick I had up my sleeve that I could show them. And I'd say that all I was doing was paying attention." He laughs and says, "Then most of them would say, 'Oh, I was hoping you knew of some other way I could learn this stuff.' "

So his head became full of desultory bits of information that he says he still remembers, but hasn't the faintest idea what to do with such as how to draw parallelograms, that an isosceles triangle has two angles that are equal, and how to solve a quadratic equation.

Many of us will dive into subjects that intrigue us, while we just barely skim over the subjects that we find less appealing. But Herb had to pay the same amount of attention to everything the teachers were teaching so that he would be ready for the test, where he would try to be, as his father said, "just a little better." "I knew that's what I had to do, what I had to be, in order to get into City College, which is what I was shooting for," he says.

In high school, Herb had a teacher who, like Gertrude Ruhman in elementary school, served as his homeroom teacher, making sure he had everything he needed to get through the day. Sam Ellis, like Gertrude, became a mentor to Herb, seeing in him things that others missed, but would later prove to be true—in spades. Sam proved to be a major force supporting Herb's sense of identity and belonging to something important. Most significant, he was the school official who encouraged Herb to apply to City College. In fact, Sam called Herb after the first of two days of entrance examinations to see how the young student was doing. When Herb said that he felt so unsure that he did not want to go back the next day, Sam just smiled and said that all Herb needed was a good night's sleep, and he was sure that Herb would pass with flying colors.

With unbridled confidence, Sam Ellis conveyed the message to Herb that he could do anything he set his mind to. It was an echo and a confirmation of what Herb had heard from his parents, from scoutmaster Lionel Goldman, and from Pee Wee Reese of the Dodgers.

Still, through it all, Herb had heard two different and extremely contradictory messages during his childhood and young adulthood. First, he had kids who wanted to beat him up because he was different, whether for them that meant being blind or Jewish. He also had a school system that wanted to send him away because of his blindness. Second, he had his parents who stuck by him, fought for him, and let him know at every turn that they believed in him. And his mentors in school and the Boy Scouts echoed and amplified that belief.

So Herb had a choice of which of those extreme messages to believe in—those who doubted him, or those who were in his corner. Fortunately, he went for the corner. He leaned toward those who believed in him. And it made all the difference in the world.

In our personal and professional lives, as Herb quickly discovered, we are inundated with all kinds of messages—some that are very positive, others that are extremely negative, and many that are mixed. Which do you pay the most attention to? Do negative experiences seem to weigh more heavily for you? How can you give more weight to your positive experiences and emotions? *At the end of the day, the more we can take in and give out positive messages, the more we will be able to believe in ourselves and in those around us.* That positive belief can become the bedrock of our leadership.

Psychological Insights—Grit and Flow

At this stage in Herb's life, some things seem to take an enormous amount of determination, and others just seem to flow.

What is the connection between flow, a pinnacle of engagement that seems effortless, and grit, the ability to passionately and persistently pursue a long-term goal?

Are grit and flow two sides of the same coin? Are they separate concepts, pointing us in slightly different directions? Or is grit what is needed to reach a state of flow?

To consider these questions, let's first focus on flow. As defined by Mihaly Csikszentmihalyi in his groundbreaking book *Flow: The Psychology of Optimal Experience*, flow is a transcendent experience of oneness that we may derive when we are completely engaged in an activity that stretches our capabilities.

It is important to underscore the difference between this feeling and where the feeling comes from. As Csikszentmihalyi explains, when people first hear about the flow experience, they may assume that the lack of "self-consciousness" has something to do with "just going with the flow." To be in a state of flow, however, is quite different. As he describes it, this optimal experience involves our total engagement. Being in flow requires a considerable challenge, along with a feeling of personal control and a complete focus on a task that is believed to be important. Your entire being is involved, and you are using your skills to the utmost.

Under those conditions, we can attain a transcendent experience of oneness where our ego seems to fade away and time disappears. In this state of flow, we become one with what we are doing. When asked what they were thinking or feeling when they were in flow, people usually say, "nothing," as Martin Seligman wrote in his trailblazing book *Flourish*. He believes this occurs because the concentrated attention that flow requires uses up all of our cognitive and emotional resources.

That's why, when we enter a state of flow, it can seem as if some universal switch has been flipped. The transcendent feeling can feel effortless, almost magical. But like a magic trick, the effortlessness is an illusion. While the transcendent feeling derived from being in flow may seem effortless, preparing to arrive at a state of flow takes extensive effort. Behind the scenes, as Herb's story demonstrates, to reach a state of flow requires passion and persistence. Those are the qualities that will enable us, ultimately, to hone our skills and succeed at our personally desired long-term goals.

So what is needed to reach a state of flow, in a word, is grit. As Angela Duckworth, a University of Pennsylvania associate professor who received a MacArthur Fellowship for her work in this area, describes, "Gritty individuals approach achievement as a marathon; their advantage is stamina." Grit entails working strenuously toward challenges and maintaining our effort and interest over years, despite any and all setbacks.

Duckworth and her colleagues evolved this hypothesis after interviewing highly successful people who kept referring to grit (or a close synonym) when they were asked what quality distinguished them. Most significant, these top performers also mentioned being awed by the achievements of some of their peers who did not, initially, seem as inherently talented as others but remained driven by a sustained commitment. Equally baffling were stories about prodigiously gifted peers who did not end up performing well.

What was causing the difference? Neither intelligence nor conscientiousness could account for what distinguished individuals who succeeded from those who did not. The something else, which Duckworth and her colleagues uncovered in this and other studies, was grit, a never-yielding, passionate form of self-discipline focused on a long-term objective. This extreme persistence can fuel our efforts. So, the more grit we have, the more time we will spend on a chosen task, and those hours spent do not just add up, but they multiply our progress toward our goal.

This brings us back to the connection between grit and flow. Allow me to illustrate how they connect by sharing a story that Roger Staubach told Herb and me when we interviewed him for a book we coauthored about the qualities that drive individuals to succeed.

Known as "Captain Comeback," Staubach was the quarterback who led the Dallas Cowboys to two Super Bowl victories. He understood flow. Known for thriving under pressure, he called upon something deep within himself in the last few minutes of a game, particularly when his team was behind. Twenty-three times he led the Cowboys to victory from fourth-quarter deficits. One of the most memorable instances occurred with 30 seconds left on the clock. Against all odds, his go-for-broke, hope-and-pray throw has now entered the vernacular as the Hail Mary pass. His description is clearly about being in flow.

At midfield, behind by 4, with the cold Minnesota wind blowing at him, he took the snap, pump-faked left, then turned to his right and fired the ball deep down the field, aiming for his wide receiver, Drew Pearson, who was completely shadowed by a Viking defender. Then Staubach was hit, so he didn't see Pearson make a spectacular catch, then, with the ball wedged between his right elbow and right hip, sprint into the end zone, sending Dallas to another Super Bowl.

After the game, when asked how it happened, Staubach replied, "I closed my eyes and said a Hail Mary."

What was it like for him being inside that moment? "It's hard to describe," he told us. "It comes down to confidence. You have to believe in yourself, especially when people are looking to you to pull them together. They want to believe in you, so you're totally focused on being there for them." He was clearly describing a flow experience, being in the moment, losing self-consciousness, stretching his abilities, having a sense of complete mastery of his performance, with time disappearing.

Then he talked about how grit was essential in preparing him to reach that state of flow. "It was just a matter of being prepared, then letting it happen," he said. "We would practice for those last two minutes all week long. That was our drill, with the clock running. But you never knew what was going to happen until you were in the game."

So grit prepared his mind. Then his prepared mind became fertile ground for flow.

Grit, then, is not just connected to, but is the way to flow. Csikszentmihalyi echoes this when he emphasizes that the ability to persevere despite any obstacles is probably the most important quality for succeeding, as well as for enjoying life.

The connection between grit and flow is particularly important for leaders. When we have passionately and persistently pursued a long-term goal, and we are engaged in achieving it at our highest level, we open ourselves up to the possibility of experiencing a state of flow. Grit is what drives us to that point. Then, from time to time, for reasons that we still do not totally understand, when we are completely in our zone, working on all cylinders, we can find flow. Or, more accurately, perhaps, flow can find us.

So if you, as a leader, are seeking to boost your level of engagement and accomplishment, discovering that one thing that brings out your grit is a clear starting place. "Your passion and persistence will trump those who may be much smarter, but not as committed," Herb adds.

An equally significant message is for you to identify those around you who demonstrate grit, who exhibit an exceptional commitment to a particular goal. Those are the individuals you want to support with all the resources you have. Focus on identifying and developing grit in yourself and in those around you. Then reward that behavior handsomely. That's how you can send a clear message and create a distinct culture where you and everyone in your organization experience more of those elusive moments of exceptional wonder known as flow.

Questions to Ask Yourself About Grit and Flow

These questions are posed for you to consider as you create your own vision, tap into your personal strengths, and pursue your own leadership journey. Your answers to these questions will provide a starting point for considering how grit and flow play into your approach to leadership. You are encouraged to consider these questions at different times, as your answers will undoubtedly evolve and change as your leadership journey unfolds.

1. When was the last time you gave your all to anything? What was it? What did it feel like?
2. What would you want to give your all to *now*?
3. Have you experienced a state of flow, where everything was moving forward perfectly in ways that you could not even imagine? Do you have any idea how to recreate such a moment?
4. Do you have a mentor? If so, what is the most important thing you have learned from your mentor? If you do not have a mentor, who would you like for it to be?
5. Are you a mentor to someone else? If so, how does that relationship make you feel about yourself? If you are not mentoring someone now, who would you like to mentor?
6. If someone is saying something negative about you, and someone else is saying something positive about you, which do you believe?
7. Do you say negative and positive things to yourself, as well? If so, which one wins out?
8. Do you have someone who is your biggest fan? Is there someone who believes in you thoroughly?
9. Are you someone else's biggest fan? Do you believe in that person thoroughly?

Seeing New Possibilities

Advancing in Degrees

Attending City College opened up a world of possibilities for Herb, who was filled with enormous hope, dreams, and expectations. He initially saw himself pursuing law, where, as a cross between Clarence Darrow and Perry Mason, he intended to save the downtrodden, free the innocent, and then get ready to do it all over again the next day.

However, as Herb started taking his required classes in college, he was drawn to psychology—partly because he was fascinated with the inner workings of our minds and, equally, because his psychology professors were world renowned and intimately involved in some monumental changes that were occurring in the profession and in society.

Gardner Murphy had just been lured from Harvard to chair the Department of Psychology at City College. His interests ranged from humanistic psychology to parapsychology, with an enduring belief in a form of reincarnation in which our minds merge into a collective consciousness. "While heading the department," Herb says, "Gardner Murphy sent a positive and democratic message by teaching my freshman class. That is unlike so many schools where the freshmen are left in large classes to be taught by assistant instructors." Murphy surrounded himself with a brilliant and eclectic array of professors, including Ruth Monroe, who brought the Rorschach test to the United States; Kurt Goldstein, whose theories deeply influenced the development of Gestalt psychology; Anna Freud, who contributed significantly to developing the field of psychoanalysis; and Kenneth Clark, whose experiments using dolls to study children's attitudes about race became pivotal in *Brown vs. Board of Education*, the landmark United States Supreme Court case in which it was declared that state laws establishing separate public schools for black and white students were unconstitutional.

Much to Herb's elation and amazement, he got to study with all of them. He particularly enjoyed being able to imbibe their teachings and, at times, challenge some of their premises. Those intellectual debates, particularly with some of the country's most brilliant minds, stirred him. "Studying with Kenneth Clark," Herb adds, "opened up new ways of thinking about psychological experiments for me. He showed us the results of his studies—where black children were internalizing stereotypes of the time by preferring to play with white dolls—before they helped to change the course of history."

Once again, just getting to school, for Herb, showed enormous determination and independence. He would have to leave his parent's apartment at 6:30 a.m., and with his cane, walk several blocks to catch a subway, change trains twice, then walk three more blocks to get to an 8:00 a.m. class. But it was worth it because in school, Herb was in his element. Beyond being engaged in classes, he was active in student government and was one of the organizers of a student-led strike against two of the professors who were openly anti-Semitic and racist. Herb says that the students returned to classes after a week, and the following year, those two professors were no longer at City College.

Meanwhile, because Herb was interested in accelerating his learning, he was also taking summer courses at Brooklyn College. That was where he took a class with Abraham Maslow—and debated with him about his hierarchy of needs. Herb felt that it was more important to focus on the need that was most deprived. "In other words," he says, "I told him I believed (and still do) that the need most deprived is what drives an individual. So, for instance, a hypothetical college student feeling sexually deprived might just chase after every remote opportunity to have sex, to the exclusion of other fundamental needs. My message was that in order to understand someone, you have to first get clear about what is deprived in his or her life. What need are they trying to fill?"

How did Maslow take to being challenged by a student?

"As I recall, he loved the engagement, the challenge and mental stimulation. I don't believe either of us changed the other's mind. But it was exhilarating to debate with someone on that level," Herb says.

Debating with an icon is interesting to consider. As a leader, how willing are you to having others openly question some of your premises? Do you invite questions? Are you creating an environment where healthy debate is encouraged? Or are you, unconsciously, seeking to have everyone go along with your decisions?

How can you encourage a workplace that allows for healthy debate? As with most things in life, this has to do with your words *and* your actions. The key point here is for leaders is to repeat, often, their core messages. That is how those who are following you will understand that your message is vital to you. Say out loud what is important to you. Repeat it, like the chorus of a song. So, if you want to encourage a free exchange of opinions, *ask* for healthy debate. Request it in your meetings. And seek it out as you meet with people individually. Let everyone you meet know that you want and need to hear their opinions. Tell them that the vibrancy of hearing everyone's ideas is what keeps you engaged, grounded, and connected. From there how you act will tell the rest of the story. Are you really interested in healthy debate? Or do your reactions say otherwise? Do you adjust your perspective or alter your opinion as the result of something new you have heard? Or are you just looking for confirmation of your previously held beliefs? Between your words and your actions, others will quickly catch on as to whether you are seeking to create an environment where healthy debate is encouraged or whether you are more interested in maintaining the status quo. Your words will speak loudly. And your actions will speak even louder.

In Herb's final year at City College, the basketball team did what no other team has ever done before or since. It won the National Collegiate Athletic Association and the National Invitation Tournaments in the same season. "When Kentucky came to play us in the semifinals," Herb says, "their coach Adolph Rupp said his team would wipe the floor with those 'kikes and niggers.' Our coach Nat Holman told his starting players, consisting of three Jews and two blacks, to shake hands with the Kentucky players just before the tip-off. When the City players extended their hands, the Kentucky players turned away. And with that final insult, City went on to crush Kentucky, 89–50. We went on to defeat Bradley, one of the best teams in the nation, for both tournaments." Herb pauses, then says, *"Our team spirit was not just about the sport, which we loved, and it was not just about winning the championship, which was a David and Goliath kind of thing; it was also about being on the right side of social wrongs and taking a stand for what mattered."*

Challenges to our principles—what we will stand for and what we will not stand for—can occur when we least expect them. For the City College basketball team players, they were just trying to win a game. But because their principles were challenged, they ended up winning more than just a sporting event. By standing up for what they believed in, each player was able to reach deep inside of himself and raise the level of his game. The final numbers on the scoreboard only told part of the story. There was a much bigger point to be made. As a leader, this message becomes extremely important. *When you pull those around you into a cause that is noble and just, their collective spirit can transcend what they are capable of individually. That is when true leadership inspires.* By tapping into our aspirations. We are all seeking meaning—and to be meaningful. We want to be part of something that is larger than ourselves. When a leader creates a clear sense of purpose, we respond because it helps to clarify our identity—why we are here, what we, ultimately, stand for. And when we stand for something together, feeling a strong sense of belonging, we get a glimpse into new possibilities—for ourselves and for others.

That is why you want to consider leading as not just trying to get people to do something. That is managing. Leading is about getting people to do something meaningful. That is where true leadership can transform us.

After his final year at City College, at the age of 21, Herb was accepted into the master's program at City College. He wasn't quite sure what he would do with a master's degree in clinical psychology, but he felt that the extra degree would serve him well as, perhaps, a college instructor or a therapist.

Then, as he continued to learn, he decided he might as well continue on, go all the way, to be "just a little better" and get his Ph.D. from New York University. He felt that with that credential he would be able to teach at most colleges, or head up programs in social work. But at that point, he also had to start making a living. He was becoming serious with his girlfriend, Beverly Hymowitz, who already had a child from her previous marriage.

So as he pursued his Ph.D., Herb got what he describes as "a hideous job" as a placement counselor with the New York City Department of Welfare. "I was earning $2,764 a year, which even back then was nothing. I had to fill out Form 531 whenever I came across someone who I felt had promise. These were for very menial jobs. But still, I could count on one hand the number of people I placed while working there for several years. It was pathetic. Very disheartening.

"At that point, my mentor in high school, Sam Ellis, whom I had stayed in touch with, said, 'Herb, you're a natural salesperson. Why don't we start a company together? We can sell mutual funds and insurance.' So I said, 'Sure. Why not?' I needed the money. And working with Sam could be a lot of fun. So we formed the Ellis Greenberg Company, while I was pursuing my Ph.D., and I got my license and packaged and sold life insurance along with mutual funds—which, back then, was something that was not done before. In fact, if the insurance companies or mutual fund companies knew we were doing it, they would have terminated us. They were in fierce competition with each other, but we figured it was best for our clients. I also got into selling wholesale furniture, dealing with barter, arranging cruises, and all kinds of legal ways to make money."

So you were working full-time and pursuing your Ph.D. full-time, with a slew of part-time jobs?

"I had to," Herb says with a shrug. "I was living in Brooklyn, so I'd get up early and catch the train on Utica Avenue and take it to 125th Street and Lennox Avenue, where I would work all day at the Department of Welfare. Then I would head down to NYU on West 4th Street, where I was taking 12 credits a semester for three years to get my Ph.D. Then, on weekends, I would sell a bit of life insurance, mutual funds, wholesale furniture, and barter to scrape together some additional money. That's how I spent my three years, after I got my master's degree."

Always looking for a way to make an extra dollar when he was not in school or studying, Herb was struggling to make ends meet. Along the way, he got married to Beverly and adopted her two-year old son, Gary.

Then, one night when he was studying, Herb got a disturbing call that threw him into a tailspin. He was asked to testify that a fellow student at City College was a communist. Beverly Rubin (who he ran together with and lost for president and vice president of the student council when they were at City College) had applied for a teacher's license and was denied because of her "communist affiliation."

This, of course, was in the midst of the McCarthy era. It was a time when fear was winning out over reason. Many in this country were consumed with the notion that the Soviets had infiltrated our country, were operating in secrecy, and had to be uprooted. They saw communists hiding around every corner. And if someone was accused of being a communist, the person had to prove that he or she was not one. Accusations of disloyalty, subversion, or treason could be made without evidence. All that had to be said was that someone who seemed too liberal was a communist. And people could be blacklisted in the blink of an eye— which would mean that they would be virtually unemployable.

In that paranoid environment, Herb was told by an affiliate of Roy Cohn, one of Senator McCarthy's top staff members, that he had a choice. Herb could testify against his friend, or he would lose his job at the Department of Welfare. It was Herb's choice. In a meeting with Roy Cohn, Herb said, there was no way he could testify that Beverly was a communist. "She was bright, caring, socially aware, and she deserved her teaching certificate. I knew she would be a great teacher," he says. But he was very worried because he was in no position, as he says, "to lose my paltry salary." Roy Cohn told Herb that he had until the next day to either agree to testify against Beverly or the commissioner of the Department of Welfare would receive a letter suggesting that Herb be fired because he was disloyal.

As it turned out, Herb's father made custom shoes for Congressman Emanuel Celler's wife. The congressman himself was a target of attacks by Senator Joe McCarthy. Rather than cowering in fear, Congressman Celler responded to Senator McCarthy's accusations toward him by publicly saying, "Deliberately and calculatedly, McCarthyism has . . . undertaken to sow suspicion everywhere, to set friend against friend. . . . It deals in coercion and in intimidation, tying the hands of citizens and officials with the fear of the smear attack."

Herb's father asked the congressman, who at that time was chairman of the House Judiciary Committee, if he would meet with his son just to hear his story. After telling his tale, Herb recalls the congressman saying, "This is so wrong. Let me see what I can do to help with this."

The next day, Herb says, he received a call, just like the first one, from the person with the same ominous voice, but a much different tone. Herb heard, "We weren't threatening you. We were just asking for your help. Just call off the dogs, all right? Let's make this easy for all of us."

Herb replied, "I'm glad you've seen the light of day." At the time, Herb wrote a poem to himself, in which he asked, "Will I go on like the rest? Crawling from year to year, dreaming of courage, but living in fear?"

Fortunately, his fear disappeared.

Herb completed his Ph.D. at New York University in 1955 with a dissertation in which he conducted original research exploring the effects of segregated education on three groups that he identified as disadvantaged—the blind, women, and African Americans. His comparisons were made between high school and college students attending integrated schools with those attending schools for the blind, what were at the time called "all-girls" high schools and colleges, and what were called "Negro colleges." He conducted assessments at Howard University, Vassar, Skidmore, Smith, Swarthmore, Wilberforce University, Indiana University, University of Michigan, Ohio State, and Penn State. Most interesting, he discovered, after having students in these integrated and segregated schools take a battery of personality assessments, was for the blind and African American students, "integrated education had a more beneficial effect" on developing their personality strengths than those who received a segregated education.

In other words, they were more confident, self-sufficient, and sociable. Interestingly, though, "the segregated college women were more sociable than those who were integrated."

Beyond these findings themselves, what strikes me as being most significant in Herb's dissertation is his early and consistent commitment to discovering ways, through the insights of psychology, to help people who were disadvantaged. His goal has been to empirically shed light on those situations that many people define as "just the way things are." At the same time, he is interested not just in highlighting wrongs but in discovering ways to change situations where people are not given a fair shake because they are part of a "disadvantaged group." His hope, all along, has been to give an advantage to anyone who finds himself or herself in the position of being disadvantaged. In fact, he says, he used the word *disadvantaged* in his dissertation rather than the word *minority* because in many situations blacks and women are actually majorities. His concern, ultimately, was to level the playing field so that everyone has an equal opportunity to realize his or her potential.

It is also interesting to note that as a student, Herb's entrepreneurial spirit was already evident. He realized that in order to conduct this study effectively, the travel costs alone "would run into figures far beyond my ability to pay." So he turned to the American Foundation for the Blind and presented this problem—and opportunity. "Fortunately, they became interested in my project because of their desire to gain increased knowledge about the most effective ways to teach blind students. Not only did they grant me a $1,500 fellowship, which, of course, went a good way toward solving my financial problem, but they also provided me with complete access to their libraries, as well as introducing me to contacts throughout the country. In addition, the Foundation's research director, Dr. Nathaniel Raskin, provided me with invaluable insights," Herb says.

As Herb 's experiences highlight, our guiding principles take wing when they are challenged. Otherwise we are just philosophizing.

As a leader, when have your principles been challenged? Did that challenge modify or strengthen your beliefs? Are you clear about your guiding principles? As a leader, others are looking for you to express your principles out loud. Then they want to see how closely your actions match your words. To the extent that you live your beliefs, your leadership moves from style to substance. Of course, challenges can come from any direction—from your competitors, from the economy, and sometimes from your key employees. What matters is whether and how you rise to those challenges. Rather than seeing a challenge as something that gets in our way or slows us down, *the best leaders among us view challenges as tests that help define us.*

It is important to keep in mind that while Herb was writing his dissertation, the country was in a time of turmoil and transition. The fear of communism seemed to lurk around every corner. Political and social unrest was brewing. Amid all of this, controversies were raging about the inequities of segregated education. There were people who felt that "separate but equal" was the way forward, and those who felt that segregation was nothing but an unfortunate legacy of the past that had to be changed legislatively.

It was a time of extremes. Controversy was heated. Fervently held beliefs were mutually exclusive. Integration and segregation were either-ors. Divisions and debates were rampant, with much pontificating but very little listening.

Amid this cacophony of disagreeing viewpoints, some people were trying to find compromise solutions that were a middle ground between the two extreme points of view. Was there a way to find agreement, someplace that borrowed the best from both extremes? Herb says, "All of the groups were very verbal, and very sure that *they* were right, and that the other side must be brought around to their point of view. But neither group was bothering to get scientific evidence to back them up. I was most interested in seeking scientific information to demonstrate which system—segregated or integrated—was better for educating the blind, women, and African Americans. Empirically, through research and experimentation, I wanted to prove the right solution. I just wanted to get at the truth. I was not interested in finding a compromise. A compromise between scientists saying that the earth revolves around the sun and those believing that the sun revolves around the earth would not bring about a correct solution."

Then the Dodgers Signed Jackie Robinson

On April 5, 1947, when Herb was a 17-year-old freshman at City College, the Dodgers made history by breaking professional baseball's "color barrier" and signing Jackie Robinson to play for the team.

Branch Rickey, the president of the Dodgers, said he saw integration as not just the right thing to do but an equally smart financial decision. The tension and backlash from signing an African American, he knew, would be strong. But he assumed it would be temporary. And once the playing field was leveled, the game would go on to become even more exciting.

Still, with his strong social conscience and keen awareness of the historic moment he was helping to create, Rickey realized that the player he signed to break the color barrier would face enormous discrimination and would need an unusually balanced temperament. He would have to let racial slurs slide off his back in the heat of the moment, in public arenas, as he set records on the field, when he was at bat, and while he was stealing bases.

After an extensive search, Rickey felt that Jackie Robinson was the man he was looking for. He told Robinson that to make integration successful, he could not respond in kind to the abuse he was bound to receive. In order for this to work, Rickey said, they needed to have a bond and pact between them, knowing the prejudice they would be facing.

Rickey said, "I want to win pennants . . . but there's more here than just playing, Jackie. I wish it meant only hits, runs and errors—things you can see in a box score." Rickey then challenged Robinson with racist scenarios—from players to sportswriters to fans. Robinson asked, "Do you want a ballplayer who's afraid to fight back?" Rickey responded, "I want a ballplayer with guts enough *not* to fight back!" Robinson thought about it, and agreed.

The racial tension actually began inside the Dodgers own club-house, where some of the players started brewing a mutiny. Pee Wee Rees, however, in a gesture that has been immortalized in a statue, put his arm around Robinson in response to fans who were shouting racial slurs before a game in Cincinnati.

Robinson went on to become the first Rookie of the Year, and the Dodgers made the World Series that year, though they lost in seven games to the New York Yankees.

There would always be next year.

Meanwhile, Herb's team made him proud, reflecting the qualities and making the kind of decisions that he would want to be known for himself.

Psychological Insights—Courage

It is natural to think of people who are courageous as being braver than most of us. Their strength of conviction can be inspiring.

As children, we first hear fairy tales and folklore about heroes that embody qualities we hope to attain as we grow older. Most of us, of course, can remember the one word that Dorothy, the Tin Woodsman, and the Scarecrow say in the movie *The Wizard of Oz* when the Cowardly Lion suddenly feels confident enough to announce, "What makes the dawn come up like thunder? . . . What puts the 'ape' in apricot? What do they got that I ain't got?" *Together, everyone:* "Courage."

"Those childhood messages are carried with us, shaped slightly differently, as we seek our identity through adolescence and into adulthood," Herb says. Ernest Hemingway's stories, for instance, often are tales of courage, which he described as "grace under pressure."

Senator John McCain (R-AZ), however, has another definition. McCain, who was tortured as a prisoner of war for five and a half years after his Skyhawk dive bomber was shot down while on a mission flying over Hanoi, emphasized that courage is more than just the style with which a situation is handled. He maintains, "There is only one thing that must always be present for courage to exist: *fear*. Because part of courage is overcoming fear."

"We often think of courageous people as being totally fearless," Herb adds. "But courage really involves feeling fear, facing it head-on, then moving beyond it. Courage is about standing up for ourselves, for others, or for a belief."

Courage comes from following your heart, persevering in the face of a daunting challenge, or standing up for what you believe is right. Sometimes courage comes in a single, extraordinary act, when someone, in a moment of self-sacrifice, rises to the occasion and becomes a hero. Ultimately, courage is about moving beyond what you are familiar with and believing in something bigger than yourself.

Courage, it turns out, is at the heart of every hero's story.

The hero's journey, as Joseph Campbell has told us, is to face a daunting challenge, then return transfigured to teach us all the lessons learned from a life renewed.

And the lesson is always the same: the powers sought and dangerously won by the hero through his or her courageous acts are revealed to have been within the heart of the hero all the time. Sometimes we come to recognize that the loud, thunderous sound that has been petrifying us is really just the beating of our own hearts.

As Dorothy discovered by clicking her heels, she "always had the power." She just "had to learn it for herself."

"It is just a matter of facing our fears," as Herb says, "acknowledging them, then looking deep within and all around us, as we rise to the occasion, turning up the volume on our beliefs and giving it all we have."

Questions to Ask Yourself About Courage

These questions are posed for you to consider as you create your own vision, tap into your personal strengths, and pursue your own leadership journey. Your answers to these questions will provide insights into how courage informs your approach to leadership. You are encouraged to consider these questions at different times, as your answers will undoubtedly evolve and change as your leadership journey unfolds.

1. Who are you willing to question?
2. Are you able to question yourself?
3. Do you have any hesitations about questioning authority? What happens when you are the authority? Do you forget to ask questions?
4. When was the last time you faced one of your fears? What did it feel like?
5. When were you most courageous? What have you learned about yourself when you were courageous?
6. Can you recall a time when you wish you were more courageous?
7. What is your biggest fear now?
8. How do you look at an obstacle? Is it something that you are up against that seems bigger than you? The same size as you? Or smaller?
9. Have you ever been able to turn an obstacle into your own advantage?

Staring Prejudice Down

In many ways, Herb had received extremely contradictory messages throughout his life. He had been beaten up by anti-Semitic thugs and accepted into the dugout of the Brooklyn Dodgers. He had been challenged by the cronies of McCarthyism and encouraged by mentors who believed in him. But he had finally achieved his Ph.D. with highest honors from New York University, and he assumed that getting a job teaching at the college level would be a breeze.

The last thing in the world he expected was to be turned down flat. While he knew that his being blind might make some people hesitate, he did not think it would be a complete deal breaker when it came to becoming a college professor, particularly when he had all the needed credentials and recommendations and had paid his way through school by consulting for over three years with the New York City Department of Welfare.

He was primed for his next opportunity.

But reality came crashing down hard and fast.

Herb sent out 600 inquiries. Within a week, he received 85 promising responses, inviting him for an interview. When he contacted these potential employers, Herb made them aware that he was blind. And, in short order, the 85 potential interviews were reduced to three actual interviews, resulting in no job offers.

"Now *that* was rejection," Herb says.

How did he come to terms with that kind of rejection?

"I didn't dwell on it," he says. "I honestly believe that I've been able to succeed in my career—not exactly in spite of my blindness but because I was blessed with a creative mind. My parents gave me a solid sense of self-esteem, and I had some incredible mentors along the way. I have also experienced my share of failures. Quite a few of them. I tried many things that did not work out, both before and after succeeding with Caliper. So it's not so much about overcoming being blind; it's more a matter of overcoming the hurt that comes from being rejected because I was blind. Somehow I was always able to use that hurt as a motivator to try even harder."

At this point, though, he was scrambling. Really scrambling. Teaching at the college level is what he had just spent nine years since high school preparing for. It was how he saw himself. What he knew he could do well. It had never occurred to him that that door would be slammed shut.

Then a colleague at the Department of Welfare told Herb about a program that had just been funded for teaching people with disabilities at Texas Tech. Encouraged, Herb applied and was asked to come down for an interview. "So, ironically, I suppose, my blindness probably became a plus in this situation, as they may have thought that I'd be able to connect and empathize with the students," he says.

Following the interview, the college offered him a job, and he, Beverly, and their young child moved to Lubbock, Texas, where Herb became an assistant professor and associate director of testing and counseling.

While Lubbock, Texas, proved to be a bit of a culture shock for the young man from Brooklyn, Herb felt in his element when he was instructing at the college level. While teaching and advising students, he was in his zone. One study he remembers conducting with his students had to do with determining people's attitudes toward work. Essentially, they found that just shy of one-third of the people they interviewed actually hated their jobs. About half of them were neutral—it was seen only as "a paycheck." Only about 20 percent of the people they interviewed genuinely enjoyed what they were doing.

He remembers very fondly on Tuesday, October 4, 1955, telling his class, as they took their seats in the lecture hall, that rather than listening to him lecture, they were going to listen to history being made. He simply said, "This is the seventh game of the World Series. The Brooklyn Dodgers are playing the New York Yankees. If you know how important this is, I invite you to stay. If you are not aware of the significance of this occasion, you are free to go." Those who stayed understood that wherever he was, Brooklyn and the Dodgers were always deep inside of Herb, inseparable from his identity. He and a handful of students crowded around his radio, hearing, between the static, the tension that filled the field as the Yankees and the Dodgers met in the World Series for the fifth time in nine years—with the Yankees, of course, having won all four of the previous matchups.

As they leaned in, Herb and his remaining students heard that the Dodgers were ahead two-to-nothing in the sixth inning. Herb explained to his newfound Dodger enthusiasts that being a diehard fan meant you had to be prepared to have your heart broken. Then, in the bottom of the sixth, it looked like the Yankees were ready to start breaking hearts. Yogi Berra hit a pitch down the left-field line, which looked like a sure game-tying double, until Sandy Amoros, running for all he was worth, made an unbelievable catch, then hurled the ball to Pee Wee Reese at shortstop, who fired it over to Gil Hodges at first just in time to catch Gil McDougald off the bag.

And Herb and the newfound Dodger fans in Lubbock let out a collective whoop.

The final out came on a ground ball to Pee Wee Reese, the team's captain, who had welcomed Herb into the dugout so many years before. Reese scooped up the ball and shot it to Gil Hodges at first, ending the game and sending the Brooklyn Dodgers to their first, and what would be only, World Series championship. Not only had the Dodgers finally won a World Series, but they had done it by defeating the Yankees. It was like winning twice. The Bums were triumphant. They would not have to wait until next season. This was their time to shine.

In Lubbock, and Brooklyn, there was dancing in the streets.

Two years later, on what he remembers as an incredibly hot summer night, Herb received a call from a reporter who informed him that the Texas Tech Board of Directors had voted not to renew Herb's contract. Herb was stunned, since the chairman of the department had just offered him a sizeable salary increase. As it turned out, Herb was being let go because he had been giving speeches around the state on his Ph.D. dissertation, emphasizing that segregation in education could not create equal opportunities for those who were segregated. His outspoken liberal views and objective presentation of scientific results apparently offended most of the university's board members.

Fortunately, Herb was quickly offered an assistant professorship at Rutgers, the State University of New Jersey, which, of course, brought him closer to his roots. In fact, the head of the psychology department at Rutgers said the reason Herb was fired from Texas Tech made him "an even more appealing candidate for this new teaching position, and made him most proud to have him as a colleague."

"When you're in the wrong place, you can't turn yourself inside out to try to fit in. You've got to be true to yourself. You can't let them get to you," Herb says. You've got to believe things will work out for the best." Ironically, years later, Herb received a settlement from Texas Tech, which was enough for him to put a down payment on a summer home.

Saying It Out Loud

Goals are meant to be tested. They will certainly test you. But you should test them, as well.

What is a goal that speaks to your heart? Something you *really* want to do? Reflect on it. Write it down and stare at it. Let it become an essential part of you—an expression of who you are.

Then say it out loud to someone you trust. Listen to how you sound saying it. See how the person responds. Consider it a test drive. It doesn't have to be perfect, but it has to feel authentic. You can fine-tune it. Then try it again.

Rebecca Stephens, the first British woman to climb Mount Everest, told us that once she said out loud to a friend that she wanted to scale the highest peak on this planet, she was in. There was no turning back. *"By declaring your goal, you are telling other people that you are open to all the fears and, even more importantly, that you have made a commitment,"* she said.

And once you say your goal out loud, amazing things will start to happen. Doors suddenly open and possibilities unfold.

It all starts inside of you. It's an inside job.

Psychological Insights—Goal-Oriented

If two people are climbing a mountain together, what is the most important thing they need to get to the summit? Teamwork? Cooperation? The right equipment? Training?

Each and every one of those is required. Absolutely.

But, what is most important is the mountain itself.

You must have a goal.

For some leaders, the goal becomes beating the competition. For others, the goal might be to beat the economic forces that are currently pummeling their company. For leaders in retail the goal might be to create a new standard for customer service. Meanwhile, a leader of a public company may have a goal of growing by a certain percent. And a leader in a start-up may be more interested in creating a new innovation.

"Whatever the goal," Herb says, "achieving it takes single-minded focus and an unwavering commitment—on your part, as a leader, as well as on the part of those with whom you chose to surround yourself. While achieving a goal is, of course, a team effort, your team will get their signals, their focus, and their commitment from you. You need to be clear about your goal, your path, and what you need to get there."

But it is not just a matter of setting a goal; it is equally about how the goal is reached. "At the heart of who we all are is motivation, a driving force that resides deep inside each of us, and can often be difficult to understand completely," Herb adds. One of the most promising ways that has been discovered to engage our motivation is by setting goals that are specific and stretch our abilities. Then, when we focus on a particular goal, hope can become the spark that ignites our motivation.

That is where you, as a leader, want to make sure you surround yourself with individuals who have a strong belief in their own abilities to complete tasks and reach goals like you do. Psychologists call this solid belief in oneself *self-efficacy.* People with a high-degree of self-efficacy are more likely to commit themselves to difficult goals, often seeking to improve their personal best or someone else's record simply as a way of challenging themselves. Essentially, people with high self-efficacy generally believe that their own actions and decisions shape their lives; whereas people with low self-efficacy may see their lives as outside of their control.

With that understanding, it is important to realize that the goal alone is often not the point. The goal, or target, often becomes a symbol of a much larger success of which you and your organization are capable. For instance, in the early 1960s when President Kennedy proclaimed, "This nation should commit itself to achieving the goal, before the decade is out, of landing a man on the moon and returning him safely to the earth," he was responding, as a leader with a vision, to the perception that the United States was losing the space race with the Soviets who, almost four years earlier, had successfully launched a cosmonaut into space.

In a rousing speech, the president said, "Why, some say, the moon? Why choose this as our goal? And they may well ask why climb the highest mountain? Why, 35 years ago, fly the Atlantic? . . . We choose to go to the moon in this decade and do other things, not because they are easy, but because they are hard, because that goal will serve to organize and measure the best of our energies and skills, because that challenge is one that we are willing to accept, one we are unwilling to postpone, and one which we intend to win."

Herb notes, "As a consummate leader, Kennedy understood that creating such an enormous goal would define a new frontier, all while instilling a sense of history and urgency in addition to inviting participation and collaboration in pursuing a meaningful mission together."

Kennedy also knew that this ultimate stretch goal, while itself meaningful, actually was a physical representation of something enormously significant, which was the United States taking back the space race. It was a way to win the ultimate Olympic game of defeating the Soviets without firing a shot in battle. Moreover, landing on the moon was such a significant and emotionally charged goal that it left no time for doubt or debate. "The way he presented it, he assumed everyone was in. All that was needed was an unwavering commitment, know-how that would be stretched in unforeseen ways, and the all-or-nothing mettle to sign up for a very daunting challenge," Herb adds.

"The president also knew that to attain a lofty goal, hope can be the primary source of fueling our motivation," Herb says. Hope is what leaders are able to instill when all hope seems gone. Hope is that spark inside all of us that is yearning to be ignited. *As a leader, you are the one whom others are looking to—not just for the goal, not just for the road map to get from here to there, but for the hope and inspiration to keep going against all odds.*

What Is Your Moonshot?

All you need is your moonshot. Being a leader comes with the lonely realization that no one else can make that decision for you. Only you can decide the goal. Will it be lofty? Inspirational? Or just to grow your company by a certain percentage this coming year? What do you want to do?

Once you've answered those questions, it would be great if it were just that simple. What you need to do is simultaneously keep in mind that the most promising way to engage the motivation of others is by setting goals that tap into their abilities and aspirations.

Keep in mind the message from William James, the "father" of psychology: before consciously deciding to set a goal, you need to be clear about what you really want—not what others want for you, or what you believe is expected of you.

Ultimately, you have to know, on a very deep level, what drives you *and* each of your top performers. As a leader, it is about you knowing who you are, then being able to transmute that energy to those with whom you chose to surround yourself.

It all starts deep inside of you. Once you have set your goal, the journey becomes yours—and from there you can make it everyone's.

Questions to Ask Yourself About Being Goal Oriented

These questions are posed for you to consider as you create your own vision, tap into your personal strengths, and pursue your own leadership journey. Your answers to these questions will provide a starting point to consider the role that being goal oriented plays in your leadership approach. You are encouraged to consider these questions at different times, as your answers will undoubtedly evolve and change as your leadership journey unfolds.

1. What new challenge are you primed for?
2. What is your ultimate goal—your moonshot?
3. Which of your habits do you feel is most important to keep repeating? Which of your habits do you want to stop repeating?
4. When focused on a goal, are you completely consumed? Or are you able to find a healthy balance between your personal and professional life?
5. Have you ever found yourself in the wrong place? If so, how long did you stay? What did you learn about yourself by staying? What did you learn about yourself when you left?
6. When do you feel most hopeful?
7. When do you feel least hopeful?
8. How do you make others feel hopeful?

Sensing an Opportunity

While Herb was teaching at Rutgers, an insurance company approached one of his associates about a possible consulting project. Since it had to do with personality assessments, the colleague asked Herb if he might like to collaborate. Essentially, they were looking for a thorough review of all of the psychological tests available at the time to determine if any of them could predict whether an individual had the innate ability to sell.

Three months later, Herb and his colleague wrote a memorandum that basically said that there was nothing like that in the marketplace. The insurance company thanked them and paid them an attractive sum.

That's when the lightbulb went on.

Herb and his colleague, David Mayer, sensed an opportunity. There was a clear and enormous need to be filled. And this need had been around ever since someone first tried to sell something to someone else. Their research showed that there was a void crying out to be filled. "Empirically, we knew that there were not any personality assessments that could accurately predict whether someone could sell," Herb says. "All we had to do was develop our own assessment. We mistakenly thought that we could do this in a very short period of time and return to the insurance company with the newfound answer they were looking for.

"Historically, the profession of sales has received a bad rap because most of the people in the profession do not have the qualities needed to succeed," Herb explains. His ongoing studies have shown that the real reason that the sales profession has suffered in terms of prestige is because more than half of the people making a living in sales should be doing something else—for themselves, for their company, for their profession, and certainly for those among us who are unfortunate enough to come in contact with them. They are not cut out for sales. "Because these salespeople do not have a natural talent, they try to fake it, and in the fast-talking process, sell themselves, and all of the rest of us, short," he says. In their desperation to persuade, they give the sales profession a black eye. They are the reason there are so many jokes about traveling salesmen, and why there are so many negative phrases about the profession, such as "selling you a bill of goods" and "selling out."

Unfortunately, these are the kinds of salespeople whom we all seem to come across far too frequently. They can make you cringe and want to shout out, "Why don't you do all of us a favor and get another job?"

Herb and his colleague knew the size of the problem. And they knew there was enormous value in helping solve this problem, as the insurance industry's overall retention rate for sales professionals, back then, was abysmal. They were losing 60 percent of their salespeople in the first year and 90 percent within three years.

Was there a way for insurance, as well as other industries, to select salespeople who had the highest probability—the inherent talents— to succeed? First, Herb and his colleague would have to discover what distinguished the best salespeople. What qualities do they possess that the others lack? If they could identify those qualities and accurately measure them, they could completely change the selection process—and the outcome—of the sales profession.

Discovering a solution to this age-old problem, Herb and his colleague realized, could be extremely valuable. So whatever spare time they could muster, they spent together trying to find a solution or develop a personality assessment on their own that could determine whether an individual had the motivation and the drive to sell.

Meanwhile, stirring in the background of that same year, the Dodgers actually did the unthinkable. They left Brooklyn. They played their last game at their beloved Ebbets Field on September 24, 1957. "It was against the Pirates," Herb says, "but who cares?"

Taking an enormous sigh, he adds, "Walter O'Malley had become the majority owner of the Dodgers after buying Branch Rickey's shares. We all knew that O'Malley wanted to build a new stadium for the team. But it never occurred to us that he would build it somewhere else."

Los Angeles offered O'Malley an unbelievable deal, providing him with revenue streams beyond his wildest imagination. But, again, who cares?

In the HBO film *Brooklyn Dodgers: The Ghosts of Flatbush*, a story is related about O'Malley being so hated in Brooklyn after he moved the Dodgers to California that it was said, "If you asked a Brooklyn Dodger fan, if you had a gun with only two bullets in it and were in a room with Hitler, Stalin, and O'Malley, who would you shoot? The answer: O'Malley, twice!"

"The Dodgers were Brooklyn," Herb says "People who didn't live there then could never fully understand that. The love, the depth, the belonging, the meaning—for all of us in Brooklyn." Shaking his head, as if still partially in disbelief, he said, "It was a personal hurt that was deep. That kind of connection to a team does not exist today. Now teams swap players and move to new cities as easily as they change their uniforms. But the Dodgers leaving? It was like your girlfriend or your wife saying, 'Screw you. I'm gone.' We had a history that was inseparable. Pee Wee Reese. Jackie Robinson. All those heroes. All those connections. Gone. Up in smoke." Pausing, he says, "The very name, the Brooklyn Dodgers, came from dodging the trolley cars—which is what we all did to get around. The Brooklyn Trolley Dodgers was actually the team's original name. What in the world does that have to do with Los Angeles?"

Nothing.

"I felt betrayed. Absolutely betrayed. You know, how could this be? I completely gave up on baseball. I mean, you know, I certainly was no longer rooting for the Dodgers. I wasn't exactly rooting against them. I just tried to ignore them. You know . . ." and his voice trailed off, as if still feeling the pain of being scorned.

The game no longer meant anything to you?

"Yeah. I just gave it up," he says. "To me, it was a fraud. If the Dodgers could do that, then the whole game was a fraud. So I went on strike. I know sports extremely well, but, if you ask me any questions about baseball between 1957 and 1962, I can't tell you anything. I just turned my back on the game. I didn't listen to a single game in all that time. I was not interested. At all."

What changed things?

"The Mets. They started in '62, and they were the same collection of bums that the Dodgers were early on. They were a new team. They had the guts to come into New York and try to do it. And I just wanted them to succeed. I became interested in the whole makeup of the team, starting with Willie Mays. Of course, they were also opposed to the Yankees, the richest team in baseball. So the Mets were like us—the opposite of the Yankees."

The Dodgers were now just a memory, etched in time. They would always be like David, with his slingshot, looking up at the colossal enemy, seemingly without the slightest chance, but with a burning hope and a desire as big as all outdoors.

"Of course, everybody knows Frank Sinatra's song where he repeats 'New York' twice, saying, 'if you can make it there, you'll make it anywhere.' Well, a lot of people probably don't know that he also sang a beautiful song about the boys of summer leaving Brooklyn. It's called 'There Used to Be a Ballpark.' " Smiling, Herb says, "Would you like me to sing it for you?"

I think we both might get a bit too emotional.

"Well the words go, 'Now the children try to find it, and they can't believe their eyes, 'cause the old team just isn't playing, and the new team hardly tries. And the sky has got so cloudy, when it used to be so clear. And the summer went so quickly this year. Yes, there used to be a ballpark right here.' "

All those fond memories and dashed hopes. Knowing what was, and what could have been. There is a place in our hearts where childhood pains have the most difficult time fading away.

Interestingly, through the in-depth personality assessment that Herb was soon to develop, he would later be able to help the Mets with their draft choices. But we're getting ahead of our story.

For now, having moved back to the northeast, where he was now teaching at Rutgers, Herb and his colleague were spending evenings and weekends trying to develop a personality assessment that could identify whether someone had sales potential.

They would remind each other of the huge need for it. And they had already verified that nothing existed that could identify hidden sales ability.

It engaged them intellectually to pursue the possibility. Their debates were intense and far-reaching. They both had a passion for understanding what makes people tick.

They knew that sales was a psychological testing ground. In striking contrast to most corporate positions, sales provides an opportunity for those who want to operate with a certain degree of autonomy and independence. "It remains the only profession where individuals are judged according to a dollars-and-cents standard. And for those willing to sacrifice the security of a consistent paycheck, sales can be extremely lucrative," Herb says.

But why is it that some people succeed in sales, whereas others who work just as hard seem to get nowhere? What does it really take to make it in sales? Variations on those questions kept them going.

Herb and his colleague's initial premise was that if someone was going to try to sell something to someone else, he or she needed to be able to understand where that individual (the prospect) was coming from. What was motivating the prospect? Why was he or she interested in buying this product or service? Was the prospect primarily interested in price? Quality? What problem was he or she trying to solve?

To uncover the information needed to successfully sell to someone, Herb and his colleague determined the salesperson needed to start with empathy, which they would describe later in a *Harvard Business Review* article as "the important central ability to *feel* as another person does in order to be able to sell him or her." They underscored that salespeople with good empathy "sense the reactions of customers and are able to adjust to these reactions. They are not simply bound by a prepared sales track." Salespeople who are empathic are able to sense what customers are feeling, "change pace, double back on the track, and make whatever creative modifications might be necessary to home in on the target and close the sale."

They continued interviewing sales managers for insights, as well as salespeople who were at the top of their game, those who were average performers, and those who could not quite make it. They also studied the psychological literature. They were seeking a premise, a hypothesis, a psychological understanding of what qualities the very best salespeople have in common.

At that point, Herb says, "I began to introspect a little bit. Looking at myself, I said, 'Each and every time I close a sale, it's a real thrill. Not only do I want the money, but it is a personal victory. I feel great when it works. And when it doesn't, I feel lousy.' "

From there, he says, he began to see what would also be needed besides empathy. "There still needs to be the motivation to sell," he says, "and the money, though important, is not enough. In other words, everybody wants the money. But the process and the result has to be a kick."

At that point, he realized there was a dynamic going on between empathy and this inner need to persuade. So Herb and his colleague started scanning the literature for two separate assessments—one that measured empathy and the other that measured an inner need to persuade. "I didn't have the courage or the knowledge at that time to develop our own assessment," Herb says. "But I knew how to cobble together a couple of tests that were solid, reliable, and valid."

What was most important at that time was to create the assessment so that it was not easily faked. Herb explains, "We knew that when people are applying for jobs they obviously will attempt to tell the potential employer whatever they think the employer wants to hear. So most people applying for a sales position will say they would 'rather be with people than at home reading a good book,' regardless of their real preference."

So, rather than going with true-false questions, they decided to go with a forced-choice format, where applicants had to select from among four items which one was most like them and which one was least like them. "It is a format where nobody can claim all virtues or deny all faults," Herb says. "In addition, the items you do not select end up saying something about you, as well." Over the course of enough responses, patterns evolved that described the person with an accuracy that has proven to be uncanny.

It had taken them four years, but they had cracked the code and solved the problem that the insurance company had first asked them to research.

They had developed a personality assessment that could not be faked, which measured two attributes that they knew salespeople absolutely needed to succeed. They understood that these were not the only two qualities needed. But if an individual did not have those two qualities, then trying to sell would be like trying to defy gravity.

As soon as they had developed a personality assessment that could accurately measure these two qualities, they went back to the insurance company that initially hired them to solve the problem. But to their complete and utter surprise, the company was not interested. At all. Not even slightly. The person who had hired them for the consulting assignment was no longer there. And his replacement was on to something else.

Herb and David were stunned.

"We felt we were like the Wright Brothers," Herb says. "We had just invented a way to fly. But we weren't interested in building a company. We were a couple of academicians who had taken on some consulting assignments. We were hoping we could sell our invention and share a nice windfall. My goal was to continue as a professor, with a tidy sum in my back pocket. But we didn't see ourselves as entrepreneurs starting a business. We had solved a problem and wanted to sell the solution. At that point, we were both broke and looking to sell what we had just developed, which we knew could be of tremendous value."

Do you recall what you might have been willing to sell your invention for?

"You know, hey, give us $50,000 and the test is yours," Herb says, laughing at the idea now. "That was our initial notion. Still, we felt like we had a tiger by the tail."

So, confident that they had developed what was needed, Herb, in August 1961, resigned from his teaching position at a university he had moved on to after Rutgers. He and David borrowed $15,000 from a small stock brokerage firm known as Gilman and Schwartz. "They owned a company at 37 Wall Street. They were selling what was known as penny stocks. It was what used to be called a 'bucket shop.' So they lent us the money for 60 percent of our company," Herb says.

"Of course, even back then," Herb says, "$15,000 could not support two young families for very long."

Did you have a business plan, with a clear understanding of what you would do with the $15,000, and how long it would last?

Laughing, Herb says, "Business plan?" Then, he repeats, "Business plan?" Shaking his head, he says, "$15,000 was all we could get. So we went with it. We figured, this is our shot." Herb reflects, "I didn't want what happened to my father to happen to me. He invented a shoe that could help people who had a difficult time walking, but didn't know how to market it. So, he ended up with a hundred-dollar-a-week salary."

Herb says, "So we poured our hearts and souls into it, and started knocking on every door we could find. We were two enthusiastic, young guys with a vision of the future." Pausing, he says, "But nobody was listening. Nobody believed that we could do what nobody had ever done before. *Ford threw us out unceremoniously. IBM was another door we got tossed out of. General Electric. Xerox.*" Laughing, he adds, "*We got thrown out by some of the very best companies in the country.*"

The way Herb describes it, he and David were treated like heretics. They had developed a theory that was at variance with the established beliefs and customs. Ironically, the members of the establishment professed that they had a problem, but it seemed like they didn't really want their problem solved.

For the most part, whenever they could arrange an appointment, it was with the head of sales. "But most of them wouldn't even see us. We just kept calling their assistants trying to arrange a meeting. In a few cases, they would see us, but more often than not, they just saw us as a couple of young academicians with a theory and some numbers. At most, they were polite. They all seemed to be preoccupied with trying to hit their quotas, trying to beat last year's numbers, trying to make money," Herb says. The conversations, whenever they happened, all went in circles. "For months, the best we ever got was some bland, unctuous compliments. It was like being patted on the head, and being told, 'There, there. Keep trying, young lads.' A few of them accepted the notion that we might be on to something. And if it worked, that would be great. But they didn't have a quarter to experiment with us, they'd say. If, for whatever reason, what we had didn't work, they didn't want to take a chance," Herb adds. The sales leaders were under pressure to deliver. They had certain numbers to meet—without the time to experiment on something that might or might not work. So, the conversations kept going around and around and around.

Reflecting back on those early days of the business, what was his biggest challenge?

"Money!" he says, without missing a beat.

Could you expound?

"We didn't have enough money," he says. "It was a constant struggle. We couldn't advertise. We didn't have any kind of budget for marketing. Bills kept coming in for rent, electricity, phones, and such. We needed to pay our salaries. And all we could do was get the word out, slowly, one person at a time, hoping to find our first client. It was a slow, very hard way to try to be in business."

About three months into it, Gilman and Schwartz, the stock brokerage firm that made the initial investment, saw that this operation was going nowhere. So Herb and David were told that they could no longer use the office they were occupying. Unsure what to do next and feeling completely deflated, David found an advertisement for a brand-new office building at 175 West 13th Street, on the corner of 7th Avenue, that was offering three months free rent. That gave them just a little bit of breathing room. "Fortunately, the place was furnished," Herb says, laughing, "because we didn't have any furniture to move in there.

"After a while," Herb adds, "we were getting very depressed. I had two suits, which I kept alternating, and trying to keep track of which one I wore to which meeting. It felt like nobody was listening. Nobody was willing to take a chance."

Herb and David were focusing on the insurance and automotive industries—two areas where salespeople were pervasive. "A lot of our money was spent going back and forth to Detroit," Herb says. One hopeful meeting might lead to another, which would lead to another. But even when meetings were able to be made, decisions were not.

At this point, their funds had just about run dry. They had countless doors shut on them. People no longer returned their calls. And it didn't seem like they had a next move. There was nothing else up their sleeves, and all hope seemed gone.

After one last trip to Detroit, they made their rounds, were either stood up or put on hold, and finally knew it was all over. They had given it their best shot and come up empty-handed. But at least they gave it their all.

So they went to the Caucus Club, one of their favorite restaurants in Detroit. In the dark, clubby eatery, they particularly liked listening to Amy Russel sing jazz standards. "We got to know her," Herb says, "and loved the way she sang 'Fly me to the moon.' I remember, as we walked in, she started playing it for us. *Fly me to the moon, let me play among the stars.* It just seemed so appropriate, the perfect way for David and me to say goodbye to our venture." So they had a last supper together. They did it big. What the hell? They ordered a fine bottle of wine and each had steaks, as they shared stories and laughs. They toasted each other for having the guts to give it a shot. And they reminisced about how close they came to pulling it off. Then, when the bottle of wine was empty, the dishes had all been cleared, and their time was up, they got on a train that would take them back to Grand Central Station. Herb and David got off the train at separate stops and went to their respective homes, where each of them pondered their individual next steps. They figured they would stay in touch, run into each other from time to time, and always look back fondly on what they tried to do together.

Then, with timing that seemed to come from a Hollywood script, Gale Smith, an executive at General Motors, called and said he had an idea. "Let me see which division is hurting badly enough to try this," he told Herb and David, who could not believe their ears. "Sure, it was a backhanded compliment, but we were glad to take it," Herb says. "With virtually all of our money gone, we took one last train ride to Detroit to start a program with the Buick Motor Division."

Gale Smith said he was willing to give it a shot. They just needed to be vetted. So a meeting was arranged by a leading research firm. As Herb described it, "A young man came to our 'office'—the small, one-bedroom apartment on West 13th Street, which gave us the three months free rent. He spent a couple of hours with us. Then we got a call saying that we had passed the audition and were being retained for the contract." As it turned out, the young man doing the vetting was Dave Power, the founder of J.D. Power and Associates. It was one of his first assignments. Years later, the two companies would work together. But we're getting ahead of ourselves, once again.

At that time, Herb and his colleague got the breathing room they needed.

As Buick dealerships started testing the new service and experiencing the benefits of hiring salespeople with true potential, the business slowly began. There was still a lot of skepticism among the dealers. Then, to their great fortune, an article appeared in *Automotive News* hailing this new approach. With that credential, several kingpins in the automotive dealership world, including Jack Pohanka, who was chairman of Pohanka Automotive Group, and Henry Faulkner Jr., who was chairman of The Faulkner Organization, started incorporating Caliper's assessment into their hiring process, with immediate success.

As Jack Pohanka relates, "Of course, every dealer reads *Automotive News*, and I remember reading that article like it was yesterday. The article quoted Herb as saying that most car dealers hire on the basis of a personal interview, weighing factors like a strong handshake, looking you in the eye, being well-spoken and coming across as confident. They underscored that hiring based on appearance was a big mistake. And, of course, I agreed completely. But what was the alternative? Then they spoke about a test they had developed that could tell you whether someone had empathy and the need to persuade. So I was very curious. If they could do that, it would be a huge breakthrough."

So, as Jack explains, he called Herb "and we got into a very intriguing conversation about how those two qualities were both needed in ample supply in order to sell. If someone had too much of a need to persuade, but not enough empathy," Herb says, "They would come across as a bulldozer. Just like if they had too much empathy, but not enough of a need to persuade, they would come across as a customer service representative who was liked by the customer, but made few sales." Herb emphasized that what was needed was the perfect blend of both.

"While it all made sense," Jack adds, "still, I was skeptical that they could really measure those qualities with a simple test. So they offered me ten free tests. Herb said, 'Give them to ten people you know very well. And when we get the results, we will describe them to you. And you can decide how accurate we are.' "

Jack took the assessment himself, along with his sales manager, his service manager, some salespeople who were stellar, and some who were struggling. The results, he says, "were uncanny. I remember they described my older brother as 'an unguided missile,' and we both thought, 'Wow. That's so funny and so accurate.'"

As Jack started using the assessment and the word spread through the automotive industry, Herb and David felt like they were finally on solid ground.

In fact, in a short period of time, they were able to buy back the 60 percent of their company from the stock brokerage firm that had invested in them.

Now, they were free and clear.

Their new approach had found wings.

And the skies opened.

Psychological Insights—Persuasiveness

One of life's ultimate ironies is that while we may like to buy things, none of us like to be sold.

To persuade others or win them over to your point of view, you have to first understand their particular perspective. Understanding where people are coming from can help you bring them along willingly, rather than by pushing them. If you start pushing, they'll either push back or you'll push them away.

"Persuading starts with listening. Not with trying to say just the perfect words," Herb says. True persuasion is much different from the debates you see on Sunday morning talk shows when a liberal and a conservative banter back and forth about their take on some issue, person, or event. Most of the time, they are not even listening to each other. They are just waiting for a pause so they can jump in with their own point of view.

We'd be floored if the liberal on such a show reflected for a moment, then said, "You know, I never thought of it that way before. You've convinced me. I've changed my mind. I'm going to be a compassionate conservative from now on."

There is no selling going on in debates. Not the slightest hope of persuading.

Debating is the opposite of persuading. Persuading begins with an understanding of someone else's needs, particularly the unspoken ones. From there, you may help that person see something in a different way—through his or her *own* eyes, not yours.

Clearly, persuading is essential in sales.

When Herb and I interviewed David Oreck, the inventor of the ubiquitous vacuum cleaner, for our radio show on WOR, he told us his three favorite words were "I'll buy it." Those words ring loud and clear in the ears of every salesperson, regardless of how successful. Those are the three words they are waiting for. Those words can make a salesperson dance.

Equally important, as it turns out, persuading is just as essential in leadership.

Mario Moussa, a Senior Fellow at the Wharton School, shared with us on our radio show a compelling story about how understanding the motivation of someone you are trying to persuade can change the course of history.

This occurred in December 1776. With very few victories under his belt, General Washington could hardly feed and clothe his army. The winter was brutal. At the end of the month, most of the men would have fulfilled their tour of duty. There was little hope in sight, little reason to continue this struggle. The straits could not have been more dire.

"It is a pivotal point in the war when Washington was asking himself, 'How am I going to keep this army together?' He considered all his options, which were few. Then he and his officers hit upon the idea of offering an incentive to sign up for six months more of duty. So they offered the soldiers $10, which at the time was not a completely insignificant sum. Then he mustered his men together, and one of the officers announced their plan to the soldiers. Then, with a roll of drums, he asked them to take a step forward to indicate their agreement. And nobody moved. Observing this scene, Washington asked himself, 'How am I going to keep this army together?' And he takes a moment to gather his thoughts, and he then delivers one of the most powerful speeches in military history and, even more generally, in rhetorical history, saying, essentially, 'Men, I understand you've made great sacrifices, you're starving, you're freezing, you've been apart from your families, and you've lost friends. But I can't pursue the cause of liberty without you. The cause of liberty needs you, and I won't be successful unless you stay with me. I asked you for six months of duty. And I understand that is a lot to ask.' Then he paused and said, 'Just stay with me for one more month. Take, with me, a small step for liberty.' And then one man stepped forward. Then another. Then virtually the entire army stayed with him for that month."

He changed the deal. He knew how to connect. He persuaded by understanding the motivations of his men. And as a result, he changed history.

Mario added, "That month led to the next and beyond. Most of them stayed for the rest of the war. But at the point, under those conditions, six months was too big an ask. One month, however, was something the soldiers could commit to. Then, once they made that commitment, those commitments grew legs, as psychologists put it."

Herb adds, "Persuading, whether in sales, leadership, or on a personal level, starts with understanding your strengths, your potential, and your motivations. Then it is equally important to thoroughly understand the strengths, potential, and motivations of those whom you are trying to persuade."

Interestingly, in studies that Caliper has conducted across cultures, a consistent finding is that 25 percent of all people are motivated to persuade others. They have a driving need to bring others around to their point of view. The remaining three-quarters of the people have other primary focuses — including connecting, creating, and coming through.

For those who are motivated to persuade, though, it is like the air they breathe.

At the end of the day, persuasion is an art. Those who are best at it pull it off with great aplomb, providing solid information and real engagement.

But where does persuasion start?

You have to start off feeling confident in order to be persuasive.

So is persuading where you stop? Or where you start?

"Persuading, we have come to believe, is a perspective, a way of looking at the world," Herb says. It starts with believing in yourself, then trying to share that belief and seeing how far it can go. Ultimately, persuasion is at the heart of every successful venture.

Questions to Ask Yourself About Persuading

These questions are posed for you to consider as you create your own vision, tap into your personal strengths, and pursue your own leadership journey. Your answers to these questions will provide insights into how persuasion plays into your approach to leadership. You are encouraged to consider these questions at different times, as your answers will undoubtedly evolve and change as your leadership journey unfolds.

1. When you are trying to persuade people, where do you start?
2. Are you asking about their concerns? Are you considering the problem they are trying to solve?
3. Do you know what is really on the mind of someone you are trying to persuade? How do you know whether you know enough about his or her motivations?
4. How do you know when someone is ready to be open with you?
5. When you are successfully persuading, what strengths in you come through?
6. Are you able to describe your vision in a compelling way? Are you able to get others to stop what they are doing, lean in, and listen to you? How could you get better at persuading others to follow your lead?
7. Do you consider persuasion to be a collaborative process? Or are you focused on the goal of bringing someone around to your point of view?
8. How competitive do you get when you are trying to persuade someone?
9. When you are trying to persuade someone, how open are you to consider other possibilities?
10. How do you establish trust?

Seeing Far and Wide

The Tests of Being an Entrepreneur

So, with the recognition from the Buick Motor Division of General Motors, the glowing article in *Automotive News,* and some clients who were stalwarts in the automotive industry, Caliper was off and jogging, if not quite running yet.

"The first and loudest response to what we were doing came from the automotive industry," Herb says, "So there was a certain irony that we were from New York and our clientele was centered around Detroit. But we were thrilled to have any clients centered around anywhere," he adds, smiling broadly.

"Then we got our first Wall Street clients, and we felt like things were starting to open up," he says. "Jack Nash and Leon Levy, who were partners of Oppenheimer & Company, became intrigued by the possibility that we could help them select successful salespeople.

(In 1982, Nash and Levy sold their company for $163 million and started the hedge fund Odyssey Partners which also became a client of Caliper's.) But back then, in the beginning, they were probably just testing our approach and measuring the outcomes. Then eventually, the slow trickle started to flow. They became our largest client for quite a while, and have been with us for over a half-century."

At that point, it was just Herb and David who were rifling through the morning mail (remember, this is still the early 1960s, so commercial fax machines would not be introduced for several more years); sorting out the personality assessments that had come in; interpreting the results of each assessment; and calling the hiring manager on the telephone to talk about whether the prospect would fit in with the company's culture, relate to the sales manager, and succeed in cultivating existing clients, while bringing in new business. After the telephone consultation, Herb or David would type highlights from the conversation, including a description of the individual's primary motivational strengths, along with an appraisal of his or her inherent sales talents; then mail the written assessment back to the client so that they could review it and keep it for their records.

The in-depth telephone consultation became a distinct differentiation of Caliper's service. It is interesting to think that if Herb and David had been less outgoing, they might have skipped the part about talking with the client. But they developed an appraisal process that was, in many ways, a reflection of their own personalities. They both shared an unusual combination of being academically proficient, while also knowledgeable of business practices.

"Whenever the phone rang," Herb says, laughing at the memory, "David and I would both lunge for it. 'You got the last one,' one of us would call out to the other. We both wanted to talk with the clients, to get a clear understanding of what they were looking for, to glean insights into what was working for them, and to explore with them how we might help them most effectively."

Those consultations with each client also created an unusually close bond.

The thought of selling their invention was now a distant memory. They were now developing and refining a business model that, between the two of them, they could deliver in a way that created a meaningful impact for their clients.

At the same time, they were trying to grow the business.

So whenever an important meeting was arranged with a prospective client, they both attended, which meant that the work back in the office had to be caught up when they returned, and before they left for the day.

"It was 'round-the-clock," Herb says, remembering.

When Herb and David were not advising their clients on how to hire successful salespeople, they were both trying to bring on new clients themselves.

However, they were not just entrepreneurs; they were trailblazers, trying to bring science to a recruitment process that had relied on initial impressions. As they tried to change old ways, they found themselves turned away from places where they thought they would be welcomed, then, occasionally, when they least expected it, surprised by an opportunity that would open like a skyline.

At the time, *Sales and Marketing Management* was the magazine that all sales professionals turned to. The magazine published an article about these two young upstarts and their psychological approach to hiring sales representatives with untapped potential. This broadened their base and appeal beyond the feature article they had in the automotive industry. In this new article, Herb says, "We talked about how, in the hiring process, we had found there is, almost universally, entirely too much concern with external superficialities (what salespeople are supposed to look like) and not enough concern with what is inside (whether they are motivated to succeed in sales)."

Highlighting this phenomenon, an article in the premiere issue of *Sales and Marketing Management* 90 years ago noted, "Large men command attention, providing that they are physically well organized and their muscle tone and health is all that it should be. Large salesmen are more likely to depend upon their size and bluff to succeed than they are to make sure of every ounce of their gray matter. Smaller salesmen must make up for this deficiency in height and brawn by using their minds more effectively. They must either have more courage and self-reliance, more tactfulness and friendliness, or more intellectual resourcefulness."

Little had changed in the way sales managers were looking at applicants since that article was written.

Herb says, "In trying to convey our approach, we knew that what we were up against was a predominant lack of understanding that sales is fundamentally a game of motivation." He shakes his head knowingly, then adds, "People knew that what we were saying made sense and was true, on one level; but they also figured that if they and everyone else were doing it the same way for years—why change?

"This new article helped lay the groundwork for explaining our approach—which was logical and academically sound but was defying preconceived notions. What we were conveying is the fundamental belief that succeeding in sales has to with what is inside of someone. The need and pleasure of getting someone else to say 'yes' is essential for successful salespeople. It drives them, like nothing else. When push comes to shove, no one can give a salesperson the desire to succeed, the need to persuade, the ability to bounce back from rejection, and the ability to understand the needs of others," Herb says. "These are all inherent gifts that some of us have in larger quantities than others. But they are not gifts that we can neatly package and give to someone else."

Beyond expanding awareness of their concept, the article also opened the door to an article highlighting their theories that Herb and David coauthored for the *Harvard Business Review*, which appeared in 1964.

"What we were most intent on conveying," Herb says, "is that succeeding in sales has to do with what is inside you."

At this point, the idea that successful salespeople all needed to start out with at least two basic qualities (empathy and the need to persuade) was starting to gain credence. The article demonstrated the validation of their hiring approach in the automotive, insurance, and mutual funds industries. People who were recommended based on the results of their personality assessment were significantly outperforming those who were not recommended—six months as well as eighteen months after being hired.

With that validation and the imprimatur of the *Harvard Business Review*, the company had the most stellar academic *and* commercial credentials. It was a perfect blend. They were not just academicians with an interesting theory that they wanted to test. They were also entrepreneurs who were able to connect with the real problems that other business executives were all facing.

Inside the article, they also learned to face their dilemma head-on. *If they were going to be perceived as iconoclasts, as running against the grain, then they had to act the part.* Rather than apologizing for believing and promoting a concept that most executives seemed to not quite understand, they would go after it full force. Be provocative. Engage the executives in the controversy.

In that article they said that in the hiring process entirely too much emphasis was placed on experience. By looking for experienced applicants, they noted, "what is accomplished can only be called the inbreeding of mediocrity. We have found that experienced people who are pirated from competitors are most often piratable simply because they are not succeeding well with those competitors." They challenged executives to "seek individuals with basic sales potential," cautioning that "experience is more or less easily gained, but real sales ability is not."

"Prior to our article appearing in the *Harvard Business Review*," Herb says, "we were doing just shy of 200 assessments a month. After the article appeared, we shot up to about 900 a month. It was like a skyrocket."

With that, Herb and David realized they had no choice. They needed to bring in their first employee. While exciting, this was not a decision they took lightly. It meant they were becoming a real company. They would no longer be just two guys giving it their best shot. They would be responsible for someone else's paycheck. And that person would impact their corporate culture, as it were. Prior to that, the corporate culture was just two bright guys trying to make their way as entrepreneurs. They knew each other inside out, got each other's jokes, and could complete each other's sentences. But they needed someone to free them up as they continued to grow the business.

They needed time to meet with their current clients, pursue new ones, and service the day-to-day business. As it turned out, whenever they could get away to visit a client or present their concepts and findings at a conference, they both had their hats on and were out the door.

"The truth is," Herb says, "we were probably more alike than different—which might not be the ideal situation for business partners. More typically the best partners are bookends—with one being more of the outgoing salesperson and the other being a more button-down head of operations. That way, because of their strengths and natural inclinations, there is more of a clear delineation between roles and responsibilities. And that way partners might not trip over each other. But for us, at least in the beginning, it was all working."

They genuinely enjoyed each other's company. On one typically crowded subway ride, a woman, seeing Herb standing, asked David if Herb would like to have her seat. Knowing that Herb had heard her request, David leaned into Herb's ear and, speaking in a language he was making up, as if from another planet, he asked, "Obalo-goomi-santa-gablew?" And Herb, knowing where he was going, responded, "Gablooma-sokola-la-soma-cola!" Then David turned toward the woman and said, "No. He said, 'No thanks.'" In that secret language, David was playing along with Herb, letting him know that he understood that such requests, while well-meaning, were often off-putting. It was not harder for Herb to stand simply because he was blind. So he did not want to be treated a special way because of it. He just wished people could see past his blindness.

So, as they progressed from being two guys who were just testing the water to becoming an actual company, how did they determine who they would add to their team?

"Like everything we were doing at the time, it was on the fly," Herb says. "We knew we needed someone who could answer the phone in a way that was very welcoming and engaging. We also needed someone who could take dictation, then type our reports and make sure they were sent out appropriately and on time. But we were also looking for someone who could grow with our company. We wanted someone who was intrigued by what we were doing and saw him- or herself as being part of something that they believed in—just like we did," Herb pauses, adding, "That, I believe, has always been at the heart of who we are as a company. Whenever we hire somebody today, we are not just looking to fill a position, but we are looking for someone who we feel 'gets it.' We are looking for someone who is genuinely enthused about what we do. And who wants to contribute and grow with us."

After assessing and interviewing countless applicants, they hired Joan Ward as their executive assistant. "She was excellent at keeping us organized and on track," Herb says, smiling, "which was a yeoman's task." Over the course of time, Joan learned how to interpret the psychological assessments and consult with the fledgling company's clients. "Eventually, she went on to get her Ph.D.," Herb says, "of which I am very proud."

Herb's son, Mark, who was born when Herb was teaching in Texas, remembers that during these early days of the company, his dad would go to work very early in the morning. "I mean, he wasn't around much during the week. But I always found him fascinating. We would take him to the New Brunswick train station early in the morning, and, with his cane, he would walk up those stairs by himself. And I would imagine him getting on the train with no one's help, and finding a seat. Then getting off in Manhattan, and taking a subway, then walking to his office. All by himself. It was just fascinating to me," he adds, smiling at the recollection. "Then my mother would keep a plate warm for him in the oven, and he would eat dinner whenever he got in at night. It was usually quite late," says Mark, who is now president of Caliper. "I was always fascinated by his sheer determination and fierce independence," he adds.

One of Mark's earliest memories of being with his father was when the power went out in their house. "Everything went completely dark," Mark says. "It was as black as can be. My mom was there also. And I was going, 'Aaaaaaahhhhhh!' And my dad was just laughing, because he thought it was all very funny. He, obviously, was accustomed to walking around the house without any lights. So he just kept laughing, as we were holding on to him, and he led us around the house. We were slowly getting from room to room, being totally disoriented, with him as our guide. It is a very funny memory."

Mark also remembers that as his father talked about his work, early on, there was a "mystique" in the way Herb spoke about salespeople. "There was a message that gets filtered through the head of a kid that if you're not a salesperson, you're not fully whole," says Mark, who describes himself as more of a "teacher." "But there was a message that I hope you grow up to be a great salesperson one day. You know, it was a subtle message."

What can you do with those messages?

"You don't do anything with them," Mark says. "You explore your own options and make your own conclusions in life. And you end up, hopefully, doing what works for you. That's what anybody should do. We all have our messages that we get from growing up. We all have to filter which ones we want to keep, and which ones we want to say, 'This doesn't work for me.'"

At the end of the day, Mark says, "I was probably the only nine-year-old who could tell you the three qualities needed to succeed in sales." Smiling, he adds, "But I also learned a lot about business from listening to his stories about the people he met and the opportunities he was pursuing. And that opened my eyes."

Hire Every Employee Like You Hired Your First

In addition to asking entrepreneurs to describe what motivates them and keeps them going, one of my favorite questions is to ask them to tell me about the first person they hired.

I enjoy asking that because, inevitably, whether that individual is still with them or not, they recall the first person they hired with incredible fondness.

For one thing, that person meant that the new venture was really a company. It was no longer just an individual trying to fulfill a dream.

And equally important, that first person they hired invariably shared their enthusiasm, their hope, and their optimism.

And that's how the company started.

Then, maybe they lucked out and a couple of jobs came in at once. And they had to hire a number of people. And the enthusiasm was everywhere. It permeated the company.

Then something unexpected happened.

A few people left for greener pastures. And their seats were left empty.

Those empty chairs can become very scary for leaders. A sinking feeling can settle in, with the clamoring message that something is missing; efficiencies are being lost.

"That is a fear with which leaders need to comfortable," Herb says.

Otherwise, they will become overly concerned and say something like, "We have to fill those seats quickly."

And the worst thing that can happen is to fill that empty chair with the wrong person.

"It is much better to leave it empty," Herb cautions.

Otherwise, the first pessimist will be hired. Then a critic will be brought on. Then someone will be hired who is just cynical and negative about everything. Then, one day, the leader will turn around and say, "Wait a minute. What happened to my company? Why has this become a nine-to-five place to work? Where's the enthusiasm? The creativity? The energy? The optimism?"

Herb advises, "If we could leave you with just one message, it is to make sure that the next person you hire is an optimist." Optimists change everything. They change what is possible. Optimists will confirm your best ideas about what your company can become.

"Let those chairs go empty until you come across your next optimist. They are worth waiting for—because they can help grow your company," Herb adds.

But filling those chairs with pessimists will only bring you down. And they could literally bring your company down. Avoid the pessimists, the naysayers, and the critics. They are always out there. You do not have to pay to have them with you.

Instead, surround yourself with people who can lift you, and those around you. They make everything you do much more interesting; certainly, more fun; and they can open up unlimited possibilities.

Be at Least Slightly Provocative

When Herb and David were given the opportunity to write an article in the *Harvard Business Review*, they knew it could raise the profile of their company significantly. They were prepared to feature a study they had undertaken that demonstrated that applicants whom they evaluated as having sales potential significantly outperformed those whom they did not recommend.

In addition, they also saw it as an opportunity to be thought-provoking—if not outright provocative. That they paused in the midst of pursuing this opportunity made all the difference in the world for their fledgling company. Rather than just let their facts speak for themselves, they also challenged conventional wisdom. *They were bringing a perspective—a unique point of view, which helped position them as experts.*

Essentially, they said that when it comes to hiring, we are all trapped by the past. Experience is the first thing we look for, they noted. If there are two seemingly equally qualified candidates for a position and one has slightly more experience, the decision seems easy. Experience wins.

After all, they asked, how often have you come across someone who has 10 years of experience that is really just one year's bad experience repeated 10 times?

To hire top performers, the first lesson is: Do not steal from your competitors. Unless you want them to thank you.

With that thought, Herb and David had moved beyond being academicians with a great new idea to become entrepreneurs who were challenging conventional wisdom.

This is an important lesson for an entrepreneur trying to distinguish him- or herself in a crowded field. *Be willing to challenge those you are trying to help.* Tell them they've been asleep at the wheel. Shake them out of their slumber. That is how you will get their attention. Even if people disagree with your provoking thoughts, at least they will become engaged. You will have their attention. Then things can happen.

How Have Your Thoughts Evolved?

With so many jobs requiring unique technical capabilities and expertise that can only be acquired over time, do you still believe that too much emphasis is based on experience in the hiring process?

"I absolutely do," Herb says. "If it is an overstatement, it is only a slight one. Think about it for just a minute. When you're putting together a help wanted ad, what's the first thing you write? 'Need a manager—or salesperson or whatever you are looking for—with at least one year experience.' No. Wait a minute. This is a much more important job than that, let's say, 'Need five years experience.' "

"Conventional wisdom is that an experienced individual will hit the ground running. But the price can be high for taking this easy road," he adds.

The truth is, we have a tendency to think of experience in a way that is really too limiting. What we should be looking for is not direct experience, but transferable skills. It is not whether people have sold the same product or service before, but what have they carried with them? Are they able to initiate relationships easily? Can they get a client to open up? Do they know how to identify and solve problems? These are some of the transferable skills that can take an individual successfully from one position to another—and even from one career to another.

In the end, effective hiring has less to do with experience and more to do with potential.

"I'm not saying to forget about experience. Obviously it counts. But, as Aldous Huxley said so well, 'Experience is not what happens to you . . . it's what you do with what happens to you.' "

Look for what applicants have learned from what they've done. How have their experiences altered their lives, formed their philosophies, and defined who they are?

The point is to look beyond the past. Look to the potential of applicants. Do they have the same qualities that distinguish your current top performers? That's what you want to know. That's the potential you're looking for."

Do You Trust Your Gut to Make Important Decisions?

As leaders, we tend to pride ourselves on our ability to make decisions by trusting our guts. Do you trust your gut? How many times have you heard or said to yourself, "I'm going to go with my gut on this one"?

Just what is it about following our guts that helps us assess possible outcomes?

Have you ever stopped to think about what that phrase *really* means? Just consider for a moment that your gut is basically your *intestines* or *stomach*.

All in all, it's not a very appealing way to go about making a decision.

It turns out that the nerve cells in our guts are stimulated when the brain releases stress hormones in response to an uncomfortable or frightening situation. It causes a physical reaction. This is the old fight-or-flight mechanism that has enabled us to survive since prehistoric times.

So it makes sense that if your "gut feeling" is that something is *wrong*, then, by all means, you should listen to it. Our gut reactions help us get out of dangerous situations, jams, and tight spots. Fair enough. That makes perfect sense.

However, what doesn't make any sense is to decide we are going to make an important personal or business decision based solely on our gut telling us that this just "feels right."

The anxious feeling we get in our gut (or the pit of our stomach) is there for the exact opposite purpose. Our gut reaction is not there to help us feel right. It is to help us avoid danger. It is there to tell us to run for the hills. If your gut says, "Get out of here," then, by all means, listen. Stop, drop, and roll. Your gut is there to help you run away from or overcome your adversaries.

That is very different from making an informed business or personal decision about two very distinct possibilities. Our gut is not the body part we want to call upon for making a refined decision. This is where we want to call upon our intuition, which takes its signals from a unique blend of our emotions, experiences, hopes, and dreams.

When the stakes are high—and we don't have to flee or fight—we should turn to our hearts and our minds, weigh all the information we have gathered, take time to feel, then reflect upon the possible outcomes, seek counsel from the people we have chosen to surround ourselves with, then walk away from the problem, sleep on it, and leave spaces in between for our subconscious to inform us.

When you are not on the run, and you have a really big decision to make, open yourself up to using all the resources you have available. Then tap into your inner wisdom and move forward.

Psychological Insights—Taking Risks

When it comes to risks, we are all fine with them, so long as they are calculated, *right*? Calculated. Whatever that means. Get out your calculators, we're going to take a risk here.

Risk, it turns out, is defined as the potential of losing something of value, weighed against the potential to gain something of value. The emphasis is on the loss and how comfortable we are with the possibility of that loss.

Risk has also been defined as intentionally interacting with uncertainty.

We all bring our own perception to risk. Whether we are prone or adverse to risk, it is a subjective judgment that may vary from person to person. The event is the same. So what we are considering—whether it is scuba diving or hang gliding—in and of itself is not risky. Our perception, our thoughts and our feelings, make it so. *At the end of the day, we can calculate a risk all we want to. But then some of us will take it, while others will take a hike.*

As the sign says: Please enter at your own risk.

"Our level of self-esteem has a lot to do with how we measure risk," Herb says. "At the end of the day, if you have an idea or something you want to pursue and your self-esteem is strong enough, the entire world can tell you that you're crazy, and it doesn't matter. You'll take the risk, so long as your sense of self-esteem is strong enough, because you see the odds as being in your favor."

But a feeling alone is not enough. If you're just following a feeling, then you could also be one of the world's most foolish gamblers.

"Right. Taking a risk as a leader is not about being a gambler. Leaders are able to learn from their mistakes, mitigate the downside of a risk, and then take their best shot at something they truly believe in," he adds. "I'm not even vaguely interested in sitting at a blackjack table or watching a roulette wheel go round-and-round or buying a lottery ticket. Risks like that—events over which I haven't the slightest control—do not interest me in the least. But if I, or one of my colleagues, come up with an idea worth pursuing, I'm in. I want to know about the risks and consider them carefully. But when push comes to shove, those risks are just the price of entry. If we lose, they are part of the cost of entering the game. If we win, it doesn't matter."

He pauses, then adds, "Is it something that's never been done before? If so, you want to ask yourself, 'Why? Or, why not?' Is it something where we already would have a lot of

competition in the marketplace? If so, then what advantage
are we bringing with our solution? Ultimately, if the plusses
far outweigh the minuses, then I'm in. You can't go for a ride
if you don't get in the car. And you can be taking a risk just
by staying in bed—so where does that get you? What you
want to bring to the game is your sense of self-efficacy, your
feeling that you can accomplish what you set out to do. If you
believe in yourself, and those around you, and tap into those
collective strengths, then the risks you're taking are just costs.
Nothing else. So you figure out what those costs might be.
And if the worst doesn't happen, then you succeeded without
paying the costs. That's my philosophy."

Herb adds, "When I was teaching at the college level,
there were other professors who had every bit as much ability
as I have, if not more. But they didn't try to develop their own
personality assessment. Why did I do it instead of them? I
can't tell you for certain, but I believe a large part of it had to
do with my willingness to take a risk."

Sometimes we can make those risks seem bigger than they
really are. Like shadows in the night.

In an interview that Herb and I conducted on a weekly
radio show we used to host on WOR, we asked Bill
Rosenberg, the founder of Dunkin' Donuts, how he learned
to take risks and become an entrepreneur. With his wonderful, raspy Boston accent, Bill said, "I remember when my son
was going to the Harvard Business School, and he said, 'Dad,
where did you learn to do everything you did?' And I said,
'What do you mean?' And he said, 'Dad, I'm just trying to
put it all together. You had to drop out in eighth grade. But
everything I'm learning now is about what you had already
learned.' He couldn't understand what I had learned that they

were still trying to teach him at Harvard Business School. So, I said to him, 'Well, what are they trying to teach you at Harvard?' And he said, 'Case histories.' Well, I only went to the eight grade, so I didn't have the faintest idea what he was talking about. So, never having heard of a 'case history,' I said, 'So, what is a case history?' I never heard of a case history. And he said, 'Well, they go through the history of successful companies, try to figure out what made them successful, then they teach it at Harvard Business School.' And I said, 'You don't understand how I learned what Harvard is trying to teach you? Where do you think Harvard learned it? They went to people like me who started successful businesses. Studied it. Then they tried to teach it.' "

Questions to Ask Yourself About Risk Taking

These questions are posed for you to consider as you create your own vision, tap into your personal strengths, and pursue your own leadership journey. Your answers to these questions will provide a starting point as you consider how your attitude toward risk is integral to how you lead. You are encouraged to consider these questions at different times, as your answers will undoubtedly evolve and change as your leadership journey unfolds.

1. What is the biggest risk you've ever taken in your career?
2. What is the biggest risk you've ever taken in your personal life?
3. Do you think about those two risks differently?
4. What is the last risk you've taken? What did it feel like?
5. Are you ready to take another risk? If so, what matters to you so much that you are willing to take that risk?
6. If the odds are 50-50, do you believe they are in your favor?

Never Being Satisfied

With the publication of the article in the *Harvard Business Review*, the fledgling company took off. With their first employee coordinating the office, Herb and David were no longer just chasing after the next opportunity, while trying to come through for their current clients and, occasionally, catching their breath. They now had time to concentrate on innovative ways to improve their premiere service, anticipate the needs of their clients, and consider how their company might evolve.

At this point, by helping to solve a perennial problem that had plagued companies since commerce first began, they had found a niche in the marketplace for which they were becoming known.

While it was still far from perfect, they had discovered a way to help companies identify people who were cut out to truly connect with and persuade others—and avoid hiring people who did not possess these qualities needed to succeed in sales.

"At the time," Herb says, "with President Kennedy's announcement that we would land an American on the moon before the end of the decade, it created a world of possibilities. All of a sudden, everyone was asking, 'If we can put a man on the moon, why can't we do this, that, or the other thing?' That spirit of 'Why can't we do this? What is to stop us?' filled the air. It was a very exciting time in which everything seemed possible."

Herb pauses, then adds, "Take that backdrop, and couple it with the notion that, for better or worse, I have never been completely satisfied—at least, not for too long. I guess that created a dynamic where I was always trying to be 'just a little better.' So, as we were advising companies on who they should hire for their sales positions, I realized that, while we were helping companies increase their batting average significantly, there were some cases in which we were missing the mark. And, that's what I wanted to dive into." He adds, with an intensity that still prevails, "Why were some people with empathy and persuasive skills not making it in sales? There had to be another ingredient. What were we missing?"

As Herb interviewed some of the sales leaders he was working with, and reviewed some of the psychological assessments of people they had recommended who did not quite make it in sales, he had countless conversations with his business partner David. "We were missing something," Herb says. "But I wasn't sure what. I just couldn't figure it out." Then he started looking within himself, exploring his own thoughts and feelings about sales. That is when he came to a realization. "I was focusing on how people who had a desire to persuade others needed to have a positive sense of themselves. And that is definitely needed," he says.

"But sales, like sports, is also a game of rejection," he adds. "In baseball, a batter who gets a hit one out of every three times at bat could end up in the Hall of Fame. So, what is as important as the hit is what happens to that batter on those two-out-of-three times when he strikes out. Does he take it on the chin? Does it get him so far down that he sinks into a slump? Or does he view it as just part of the game? Can he just shrug it off and get himself mentally prepared for his next time at bat? He can't take it personally," Herb says. "That will send him into a tailspin. It's the same thing in sales. Except there the odds are even more against you. In most sales situations, it is far fewer than one out of every three opportunities that you close a sale. So how does a salesperson handle that rejection? That was my 'aha' moment. Could we discover a way to measure how someone would handle rejection? That's where we needed to go."

There was one sales applicant in particular who still sticks out in Herb's mind. He had recommended this applicant to a client because he had outstanding empathy and was driven to persuade. "Sure enough," Herb says, "he started out like a whirlwind. Shortly after the training period, it looked like he was going to become one of their star performers. Three months later, however, all of his progress came to a grinding halt." As it turned out, this individual had a strong enough need to persuade, so he closed some early sales. But when the rejections started to kick in, he was not able to look at the situation and realize that it was just the statistics finally catching up with him. "Instead," Herb explains, "he saw the rejections as the truth finally being told. He saw the early success as simply a fluke, and the failures as a true representation of himself. Then, as he desperately tried to turn his situation around, he pressed too hard and drove away prospects that he would have sold earlier. The more he pressed, the more he failed, and the more he failed, the more he came down on himself, spiraling, unfortunately, to his own undoing."

In order to succeed in sales, Herb saw, you had to view rejection differently from the majority of people on this planet. Most people, when they are rejected, say to themselves, "Well, that wasn't a whole lot of fun. I don't think I'm going to try that again."

But successful salespeople, Herb found, view rejection as a learning experience. It is not to be taken personally. Rather, when they are turned down or lose a sale, they are walking away saying something to themselves along the lines of, "I understand what just happened. I didn't know enough about my prospect, or my competition, or the market-place." And if they could, they would go through a revolving door and replay the situation all over again—with a different ending this time.

"Resilience, quite simply, is an individual's ability to feel good enough about him- or herself, so they can accept rejection not as a personal affront but as part of life," Herb says. "Someone with resilience has the ability to leave the rejection behind and go on from there. Those who accept themselves, who have a strong enough sense of resilience, operate freely and fully, allowing themselves to function at or near the top of their capacity."

As Herb discovered a way to measure resilience with the same accuracy and depth that he knew how to measure empathy and persuasiveness, he dramatically improved his firm's ability to predict whether someone could succeed in sales.

From there, as their work expanded beyond the automotive, insurance, and mutual funds industries, Herb says, "We soon learned that being able to sell was just one piece of the puzzle. Although all sales jobs involve, at their core, the ability to persuade, the breadth of these jobs is virtually limitless."

Sales jobs range from quick-closing, hard-selling, short-term, commission-only positions to the opposite extreme, where the persuasive element is much more subtle and takes place only a few times a year at the end of a long process. Similarly, many sales positions require little technical background, while others require the salesperson to be a technical expert in a particular product or service. Some sales jobs presume that the individual customer will buy once and likely never again, while in most other sales situations, a one-time-only buyer would be disastrous.

"As we got deeper into the sales process, and closer with our clients," Herb says, "we understood that we needed to ask a lot more questions in order to understand the requirements of the specific sales role, and, therefore, the personality attributes required for an individual to fill that role successfully." He adds, "This is when we coined the phrase 'job matching,' which, essentially, was a shorthand way of connecting the actual requirements of the job with the personality qualities needed to succeed in that position."

They were adding science to a hiring process that prior to that had gone on nothing more than first impressions and gut reactions.

"Even today," Herb says, "when we ask a manager what the three most important responsibilities are for someone reporting to him or her, then we ask the person reporting the same question, we rarely get the same three answers from both the manager and the person reporting to that manager. Then, on those rare occasions when we do get the same three responses from the manager and the person reporting to him or her, it is *extremely* seldom that we get them in the same order of importance."

That is amazing when you stop to think about it.

How in the world could managers hire for a position, let alone manage expectations, if there was not clarity and consistency on the three major responsibilities for that position?

The implications were far-reaching—for Caliper, as well as for the clients with whom they were working.

Herb's company was quickly moving beyond where they started.

As he began to broaden and deepen the personality assessment, he realized that identifying two of the qualities that were required to succeed in sales was just the start.

Herb was now asking fundamental questions that got at the heart of what drove people in all walks of life. By assessing and understanding the motivations of people in the workplace, he was gleaning a clear understanding of the requirements of not just sales, but also customer service, technical, management, and leadership positions. He and David were moving beyond sales and becoming poised to help companies improve their ability to hire and develop top performers in every position, and at every level. They were gaining key insights into why some companies succeed and others flounder.

By identifying best practices, they were starting to evolve from being a company that assessed potential to one that could advise clients on all of their human resources needs—from hiring and developing top talent to team building to succession planning to leadership development.

Lessons for First-Time Managers

Interestingly, as Herb and David hired their first employee, they both became managers for the first time as well. They found that supervising someone else is a new responsibility and provides more than a few new and interesting challenges.

Before Herb and David were both leaders and top performers in their organization—everything started and stopped with them. But now things were going to be different.

They needed to learn the fine art of managing.

While there are many books, articles, and seminars on what makes an effective manager, studies show that most people in management positions have little or no management experience or training before taking on their current role. In addition, according to the Bureau of Labor Statistics, more than half of workers who move up to supervisory, managerial, or executive positions came from other roles inside the same firm.

At the end of the day, a company's productivity and ability to retain top performers depends largely upon the skills of its managers. But *first-time managers often have misperceptions about what it means—and what it takes—to be a successful manager.* There is a huge change in both mindset and behaviors when moving from doing work oneself to achieving results through the work of others.

"The most common mistakes of new managers tend to fall into two categories," Herb says. "They are either too tough or not tough enough. It is a very difficult balancing act."

Managers who are "too tough" in their approach to supervising others rely on their authority to get things done, Herb explains. "They might say, 'I'm simply going to tell people what to do, and if they just do it the way I've always done it, they're going to be fine.' But it rarely works that way."

On the other hand, managers who are "not tough enough" may feel uncomfortable with their new authority. They may be managing people who were formerly their peers and still want to be friends like they were before. But, when someone moves from peer to manager, the rules change. "They are now in a position where they have to hold not just themselves accountable, but others as well. And, sometimes they either don't know how to do that or don't want to," Herb says.

"Among the most important lessons for a new manager is realizing that people don't want to be told what to do and how to do it—they want to know 'why.' The people in your organization want to know they are part of something that is meaningful. Let them know how their assignment or project fits into the company's larger goals and overall objectives," he adds.

What are the personality attributes needed to succeed as a manager?

"You need to be bright enough to be able to think on your feet," Herb says. "You also need to be assertive enough to be able to push an agenda forward. Of course, you need to be persuasive, so you can bring others around and create consensus. In addition, you need to be resilient enough to rebound from difficult situations that might arise. You also need to be self-motivated, as well as have what we call *external structure*, or the ability to organize thoughts, work, and people. And last, but not least, you need to have a high sense of urgency, or a need to get things done—*now*, rather than later."

How are those personality attributes translated into behaviors?

"What you see in effective managers," Herb says, "are individuals who know how to establish goals, priorities, and expectations for their team. They know how to persuasively sell ideas while gaining support and buy-in from others. They recognize problems, issues, and opportunities. They are also willing to make tough decisions, and know how to leverage resources effectively."

What are some other pieces of advice that can help people to become successful managers?

"First and foremost," Herb says, "when someone takes on a management role, it is often in addition to his or her day-to-day responsibilities. So it can be overwhelming. It is important to discuss with your manager what is expected of you in this new role so that you can work toward achieving realistic goals.

"It is also important to know that you have much to learn and be open to learning from your team," he adds.

"Communication is also vitally important. *In the beginning, don't be afraid of overcommunicating.* It is better to state what you think is obvious than to find out later that your team did not understand your expectations. Also, listen. Invite and welcome questions and insights from others. Make sure they know that you are there to listen to their concerns and ideas, as well as to help provide solutions.

"And give praise often," Herb says. "No one will ever complain that you said 'thank you' too often. *Provide feedback that is real, honest, and positive.* Praise individuals formally as well as part of what you do every day."

Another cardinal rule is to *address concerns immediately.* "Whether behavior or performance related," Herb says, "it is important to address concerns before they become a bigger problem and affect the team and its productivity. Address these concerns one-on-one, in a way that is honest, straightforward, and highlights a place for improvement."

Along these lines, you also need to recognize that you are now there to be a coach. Your professional growth as a manager starts or stops with how well you can allow, encourage, and help develop someone else's growth. Become the mentor you always wanted to have. Establish trust, and others will seek out your advice.

One of the most difficult challenges for new managers is learning how to manage conflict within their team. "Conflict is not bad," Herb says, "it is necessary to drive ideas and creativity. Team members should absolutely feel comfortable stating their opposing viewpoints. But it is also important to realize that some members of your team, including yourself perhaps, may have a low tolerance for conflict. So they will avoid it, which can shut down ideas and negatively affect your team's dynamics. In many ways, conflict can have a Goldilocks effect. How much is too much? How much is too little? What is vitally important is to understand the nature of the conflict within your team. Then allow it, so long as you can move past it, keeping it light and healthy."

Equally important is to manage priorities. As a new manager, in order to make sure that your larger goals are achieved, you need to manage day-to-day priorities. It is your job to keep everyone on your team on track, whether you are managing a project, time, people, or resources. It is a matter of looking far and wide—keeping your eye on the big picture, while focusing on what is most important right now. All the while, you have to keep in mind that we all have a tendency to leave until later our least-favorite things-to-do.

How do you, as a new manager, measure the progress of someone on your team?

Herb says, "I always believe in having, at the most, three key initiatives for someone on your team to work on. Sometimes it is just one. Keep it simple, straightforward, and measurable. And be clear with each individual on your team what their goal is, and how what they are doing contributes to the overall goals of your organization. That way everything is in the open, and you are perceived as fair. Then you can measure progress, and how close the person is to obtaining his or her individual goal. As a manager, it is letting everyone on your team know that you are in it, together, with them, sharing ideas, concerns, and accomplishments. And that *they* can make a difference. Let them know how important they are, while always using the word *we*."

In keeping with this advice, it is most important to honor yourself and to honor those with whom you chose to surround yourself. Create a tone of continual learning, for yourself and for those around you. As if it is your mantra, repeat often and with conviction that you are committed to everyone in your organization constantly finding ways to keep learning and getting better. "Regardless of how well things may be going right now, the future is around the corner, always presenting new challenges and opportunities," Herb says. Staying the same is a sure way to fall behind.

One final piece of advice for a new manager is to consider what you will do when the first mistake happens. Because it will, so be ready for it. Keep taking risks and encourage everyone on your team to do the same. Realize that there will be mistakes and that's OK. But, more important, realize that the first time a mistake occurs, whether it is something that you happen to cause or someone on your team inadvertently caused, how you handle it will set the tone for how you are perceived afterward.

So, be ready for things to go wrong. But don't get upset because it happened on your watch. Let your team know that you are all in it together. Consciously get ready to shrug your shoulders. And smile. Allow mistakes to happen—so that you can learn from them. That is the only way you will see new and innovative ideas flourish.

On a final note, Herb says, "One of our clients, who heads up human resources for a Fortune 500 Company, told me that she reminds the managers in her company that they go home to dinner every night with everyone they work with." That's a funny thing to think about. That accounts for a lot of dinners we may not realize we are having.

But, as a manager, you are, in fact, part of the dinner conversation with everyone on your team. Whether you set a wonderful tone or whether you are, in fact, driving people absolutely crazy, every day, there is a new example of who you are and how you come across.

Are you fair? Inconsistent? Moody? Inspiring? Indecisive? Clear on your vision?

People will either need to recover from being with you or want to share how fortunate they feel to be among the few lucky ones who have a truly great boss.

In the end, the message is to believe in yourself—as you believe in those with whom you surround yourself. And let them know that. Say it out loud. What happens when someone believes in you? You excel. You stretch. And, sometimes, you even surprise yourself.

What Are You Practicing?

Musicians have a saying that if you don't practice for one day, you'll notice. If you don't practice for a second day, other musicians will notice. And if you don't practice for a week, the audience will notice.

So, what are you practicing now?

Musicians can practice running scales from the top to the bottom of their instrument's range. Or, they can practice rhythmic challenges, new concepts, or work on particularly difficult pieces that require enormous dexterity.

The notion of practicing is something that leaders could learn a lot about by listening to musicians.

So, what is it that *you* are practicing?

This is not something that most leaders think—or even talk—about. We usually just do whatever it is we're doing. As leaders, we live more in a world of doing than practicing.

But musicians, regardless of how accomplished they are, always practice.

That's interesting to think about.

What would be different if you were practicing? What would you practice? Would it be communicating your vision? Implementing your plans? Measuring progress? Recognizing success? Mentoring others? Honing your intuition? Staying focused on what is important? Being more flexible? Getting more in tune with yourself? Connecting more with others?

What are you practicing? It's a question worth asking yourself.

Listen and learn from musicians.

You can take your leadership skills to a whole new level by figuring out what you are going to start practicing.

Today. Tomorrow. Next week. And beyond.

Psychological Insights—Never Satisfied

"I can't tell you why," Herb says, "but I am never satisfied. At least not completely. Or for a long period of time."

That is a very strong, unwavering statement. Is it that inability to ever be completely satisfied that keeps you constantly striving?

"I am just always thinking and feeling that there is more to be done, more we can do." He pauses, then adds, "I understand that others need a goal, and that they get very enthused and animated as they get closer to that goal. Then they are over-the-top if they reach their goal or surpass it. I understand that, but it is not for me. It's not what I need. When I am passionate about doing something, that's all I need. I just start off in that direction and keep going and going, as far as

I possibly can. Then I'm trying to figure out how to get just a little further."

Does that sense of never being satisfied come from rooting for a team that always came up just a little short—except once, then they left shortly afterward?

"I can't blame everything about me on the Dodgers," Herb says, laughing. "For me, life is just about always striving, always trying to be just a little better. It's not being better than someone else. It's just trying to be a little better for myself."

I'm reminded that your father told you that you had to be "just a little better" when you were very young.

"That's true," Herb says, reflecting. "I just have to keep constantly moving forward. Always finding new journeys because I cannot settle. I don't have the slightest interest in settling. Not in the least. It is not in my nature. And I can't settle for anything less."

For leaders, that message of always striving and never being completely satisfied is worth pondering. As Barry Schwartz, professor of social theory and social action at Swarthmore College, points out, "Who do you think is happier, an athlete who wins a silver medal in the Olympics (second place) or an athlete who wins a bronze medal (third place)?" While it might seem that the silver medalist would feel happier than the bronze medalist, on average it turns out not to be true. Why? Because as the winners are standing on the platform, the silver medalists is thinking about how close he or she came to winning the gold. More often than not, the athlete is thinking, "If I had just done a little more of this or a little less of that, I could have made gold." The bronze medalists, however, are standing on the platform thinking about how fortunate they are, how many people they just barely beat to make it up on the podium. As Schwartz points out, ironically, the bronze medalist *feels* more of a sense of triumph, accomplishment, and satisfaction.

It is an interesting paradox for leaders, as well as any high achievers. Must we always be reaching for the gold? And if we become satisfied, is it a sign that we are bowing out of the race? Where does your satisfaction reside?

Questions to Ask Yourself About Being Satisfied

These questions are posed for you to consider as you create
your own vision, tap into your personal strengths, and pursue
your own leadership journey. Your answers to these questions will provide a starting place for you to consider how
your attitude about being satisfied plays into your approach
to leadership. You are encouraged to consider these questions
at different times, as your answers will undoubtedly evolve
and change as your leadership journey unfolds.

1. What drives you?
2. Are you always challenging yourself?
3. When are you satisfied?
4. When are you not satisfied?
5. Is "good enough" ever good enough for you?
6. Can you find that precarious balance between always striving, while savoring your successes?
7. Are your sights always set higher?
8. What is your ultimate dream? What do you really want?
9. What are you willing to do to bring that dream alive?
10. How can you connect your potential with your dream?
11. What would it be like to live your dream?

Welfare to Work

Helping anyone who is in any way disadvantaged is at Herb's very core. So when President Johnson declared a War on Poverty during his State of the Union Address on January 8, 1964, Herb was in. With both feet.

"The president was responding to a national poverty rate that was nearing 20 percent," Herb says. "With a vision of a Great Society, President Johnson wanted to expand our government's role in education and healthcare. The policies he was introducing reminded me of what President Franklin Roosevelt was doing with the New Deal, when I was a child," Herb adds. "I was also reminded of my job at the Department of Welfare, where I felt frustrated and ineffective, I was seeing the need, but unable to do anything to make a difference. Contributing to President Johnson's War on Poverty, I believed, was my chance to take all that I had learned and developed and help create a new, more positive outcome for people who had potential but could not see a way out of their situation. I saw it as an opportunity to hope-fully reinvent a new future for many people."

It was as though his past was coming back with another chance.

"Taking the president's lead, Congress passed the Economic Opportunity Act, which established the Office of Economic Opportunity. That's the door where I went knocking," he recalls.

It was there that Herb met Sargent Shriver, known as the archi-tect of the War on Poverty, who became the first director of the Office of Economic Opportunity. Herb would also get to know Robert Kennedy, who, as the attorney general at the time, was very interested in the promise of this new program. "Sargent Shriver believed in us and gave us an initial grant of $198,000 to staff an office and conduct our first project in San Juan, Puerto Rico, called Programa de Nuevas Oportunidades, which translates into 'New Opportunities Program.' Our successful placement of what were known as 'chronically unem-ployed' individuals in that program enabled us to get an additional grant for the next year. Through our in-depth assessment of an individ-ual's potential, we ended up matching over 350 hard-core unemployed individuals to productive sales jobs in the San Juan area. They wound up working for Shell Oil, phone companies, and newspapers. They were getting real jobs that helped set their life in a new direction."

Herb dove into this project and gave it all he had. "David kept the day-to-day stuff moving forward, our more traditional work, if you will, while I focused on the potential and growth of this project. I had to hire people, train them on how to interpret our assessment and consult with clients, find companies willing to take a chance on this new approach, and create a network of applicants who were looking for a new beginning. It was around-the-clock."

*Where would he find people who had the ability to consult
with clients?*

"I was always looking, always trying to piece it together. I heard a blind musician playing piano in a club in Queens. So, as I got to know him, I sensed he could read and connect with people really well, and he spoke Spanish. Our assessment confirmed all that and more. So Angelo Henri came to work with us on this project, and stayed on as a consultant with us afterwards for quite a while." Pausing, Herb adds, *"That was one of my favorite parts of being an entrepreneur: sensing someone's potential and being able to do something about helping him or her realize that potential."*

He adds, "Along the way, I had to 'sell' or convince executives of companies we had never worked with in Puerto Rico that it was worth taking a shot to hire someone who had never held a job where they earned more than $1,800 a year—but who we had determined had real potential." Shaking his head, he says, "It was a hard sell. No doubt about it. Sure, I would tell them about the tax breaks they would receive. And I would try to appeal to their social conscience, but I had to prove it would work. Fortunately, we began building stories early on. For instance, we had hired a babysitter, Maria. But after assessing her, we saw that she had sales and even sales management ability. So we put her through two weeks of job readiness training. She was then brought on by a large mutual fund sales organization that put her through their sales training program. She became the first woman to be licensed to sell mutual funds in Puerto Rico, and six months after her initial training, she came back to the program to hire five people to work for her," Herb says, smiling. "So we lost a babysitter, but gained a wonderful success story.

"On the heels of that program, Leon Levy and Jack Nash asked if we could help them hire people who had never had a job before for Oppenheimer & Company. They were impressed by the work we had done in Puerto Rico, and both of them had such a strong social conscience, which I admired greatly. At this point we were expanding beyond sales positions to virtually every position—including clerical, technical, administrative, professional, managerial, and leadership. Interestingly, the most difficult thing for us at that time was finding applicants who were willing to think of themselves and their possible futures in a more positive light. I remember, it actually took a lot of coaxing and convincing to get applicants to open up to new possibilities for themselves."

Toward the end of the 1960s, Caliper received a $2.88 million grant, funded by the United States Department of Labor and the National Alliance of Business, to help people move from welfare to the workplace in New York City. "With that, we had to move our offices from the little apartment at 175 West 13th Street to 404 Fifth Avenue," Herb recalls. "At that point, we went from having a dozen people to 96."

*That is transformational for a company. How did that change
his approach to leading, let alone the culture of this very
young company?*

"Well, we had an advantage in that we knew how to assess everyone's potential, so that helped us hire people who had the inherent talent and would fit in with us," Herb says, smiling. "I also believe that because of the nature of the work we were doing—helping people in an innovative and meaningful way—that the people who wanted to work with us were very committed and focused."

Herb adds, "Our success that first year led to the fastest 4.69 million dollars I have ever received in my life. I walked into the Department of Labor office on 9th Avenue in New York, and 15 minutes later, I got a grant that was nearly double the size of the original grant to continue the program for another year. Over the course of those two years, before administrations changed and the War on Poverty was being dismantled, we placed over 3,600 'hard-core unemployed people' in 55 job categories with 52 New York area companies."

Helping people move from welfare to work connected Herb's past with the promise of a new future. Strands were connected—from rooting for the underdog, to experiencing prejudice as a child, to being beaten up on his way to school, to writing his dissertation about disadvantaged groups, to trying, fruitlessly, to help people at the Department of Welfare, to being an integral part of the War on Poverty. Ironically, while he had initially pursued a request from an insurance company to help them find a way to hire more effective salespeople, he ultimately found a way to help people from all walks of life discover their true potential.

For Herb, everything was expanding—his company as well as his vision of what could be. "We assessed over 7,000 people in New York, and placed over half of them," he says. "What was exciting was they were for every job under the sun and the turnover was very low. Most of them succeeded. Not all of them, surely, but most of them, which was unheard of. And, to make things better, some of the success stories were truly inspiring," he says, nodding, as if in agreement, as he remembers.

Among his favorite stories is of Georgie, a 22-year old man from Harlem, whose only previous employment was some deliveries and scattered odd jobs. When he was assessed, it was discovered, as his counselor put it, "that Georgie could sell sand in the Sahara Desert."

Herb recalls, "We told Georgie that we wanted to refer him to a life insurance company that was participating in our program. He literally laughed and asked, 'What's life insurance'? He totally ridiculed the idea of being a salesperson, particularly the idea of attempting to learn a profession about which he had absolutely no knowledge. It took several counseling sessions to finally get Georgie to laughingly admit that maybe he did have some sales ability. 'I guess I can sell,' he said, as he realized how easy it was for him to convince his friends to go along with some of his ideas. Georgie went for an interview and was hired on the spot. And, within two years of acquiring his license, Georgie became a member of the Million Dollar Roundtable."

There is a final success story from this program, which is perhaps closest to Herb's heart. A young man named Ralph fell asleep while taking the personality assessment early one morning. "We were concerned that drugs might be involved," Herb says, "but, as it turned out, Ralph had tended bar until 2 a.m. that morning and was simply exhausted at 7:30 in the morning. In any case, this assessment indicated that he had management ability. There was one problem, however. He had a rap sheet, and it was a rather extensive one. There were no violent crimes, but there were enough arrests and convictions to block him from consideration for most companies. Gimbels, the department store, however, had some very good experiences with a number of people that we had recommended to them, so they took a chance on Ralph. As it turned out, he received several promotions within two years. He was even in a position to hire some people from within our program. And when my daughter was born, my wife and I received a dozen roses from Ralph, with a note saying, 'To a new life, from a life you saved.'"

Through his in-depth approach to uncovering an individual's potential, Herb helped over 4,000 "hard-core" unemployed individuals move from welfare to work for the first time in their lives. "This, to me, remains the most significant experience of my professional life," Herb says. "We were able to provide conclusive evidence that the unemployed and underemployed are an untapped and exceptionally rich source of talent. Not only did the people we placed succeed, but many were promoted and moved on to managerial positions. And in the follow-up after two years, it was found that fewer than 3 percent had been terminated because of their inability to do the job. These programs proved my hypothesis—that ability exists across the population, regardless of what individuals have or have not done in the past. What matters is what someone *can* do, not what they *have* done."

Herb concludes, "Ultimately what this means is that there is no shortage of candidates with the potential to succeed. What leaders and managers need to do is open themselves up to looking in places where they might not have before. Throughout my life I have fought against this human tendency to limit what people can do. I strongly believe that we are not merely what we have done. We are who we can be. Don't let the past limit you or anyone around you. Be open to yours and someone else's potential.

"My strong advice," he adds, "as you look to uncover someone's potential, is to realize that you cannot give someone the right attitude. An applicant who possesses a positive attitude is bringing you an enormous gift. In fact, the best training companies we have worked with confirm that you can teach skills, but you cannot teach attitude. Whenever you come across an applicant with the right attitude and with the potential to succeed, you have found someone worth investing in because they possess the essential foundation on which you can develop your next top performer."

Hiring in Your Own Image

When you are looking to hire for an important position, how can you find someone who has the qualities you are looking for?

Maybe you could start by looking in the mirror. Obviously, you're driven to succeed. So all you need to do is hire people who are more like you. Right?

The truth is that nothing could be more wrong.

"What we all need to keep in mind is that it is only natural for us to want to work with people whom we like," Herb says. "We all tend to like people who are most like ourselves. For better or worse, it's just human nature."

That's why we are all fascinated whenever we meet identical twins. They can make people do a double take as they enter a room together. Ultimately, they are as close—genetically speaking—as two people can be on this planet. And it makes them feel special—*particularly when they are together.*

If you think about it, when identical twins see each other from across a crowded room, they know that they are with the one person on this planet with whom they have the most in common.

Liking someone who reminds us of ourselves is just human nature. We can't help ourselves.

That's why, without being conscious of it, we often end up hiring people with whom we have much in common. Maybe they have the same hobby that we do. Or there is just that special chemistry. Whatever the connection, it usually starts with having something in common.

Then we end up saying, "There's something about that person I really like. I'm not quite sure exactly what it is. But they remind me of someone I'm very fond of. Let's see. Who could it be?"

As Herb notes, "Of course, we don't want to surround ourselves with people who get on our nerves. But if you hire an entire staff of people just like you, you will inevitably create an unbalanced organization. We have to remember that a staff with all of our strengths and virtues will also share our faults and shortcomings."

So they will help us stay right where we are, not help us grow to where we need to be.

Growth

Tom Gartland, former president, North America of Avis Budget Group, shared with us, "You have to keep in mind that you are hiring someone for a certain position, but you are also hiring that individual for the future. Knowing everyone's growth potential is vital to the growth of our organization."

Herb underscores, "What you really want to know is whether a promising applicant can grow with your company. Does he or she 'get' what you and your company are about? Can you see them years from now, contributing to your company in even more meaningful ways? Are they in it for the long haul?"

How can you tell if someone has the ability to grow with your company?

"While growth is related to an individual's ability to acquire new information and view situations from a fresh perspective, it is not merely a reflection of intelligence," Herb notes. "Some people, while being very bright, are so opinionated, rigid, and dogmatic that they use their intelligence to reinforce and defend their preconceptions. In other words, they use their intelligence to build a wall around themselves, selecting evidence that supports what they already believe to be correct and ignoring all conflicting ideas and facts." Such individuals, unwittingly, use their intelligence to keep themselves from growing. "We have come across individuals whose IQ was in the genius range, but who were not capable of growing beyond their current job," Herb adds. "Being able to grow, on the other hand, involves intellectual capacity, but it also requires the empathy to understand those around them and themselves while also possessing the flexibility of mind to ponder and seek new ideas and methods."

Psychological Insights—Optimism

"Truly succeeding," Herb notes, "is finding meaning in your life's work. It is about finding purpose that goes beyond yourself—that connects you with something larger, more significant, and more meaningful."

It starts with having a core belief. And living it.

All of this leads to a big question: Does the way we view the world make a difference to anyone but ourselves?

As Henry Ford was known to say, "Whether you think you can, or you think you can't—you're right."

Are you more optimistic? Or more pessimistic?

Here's a little test to help you find out: How do you view negative things that happen? Are they happening to you? To everyone? Can you change them?

Pessimists view negative things that happen as something they inadvertently caused. They believe negative events are just the way things are. They tend to believe there is not much they can do to change negative situations.

On the other hand, optimists typically view negative events as something rare that will pass. They do not take things that go wrong personally. Instead, what optimists do take personally are things that go well. Optimists view positive events as outcomes that they helped to make happen. And they fervently believe that they will be able to continually make positive things happen in the future.

Martin Seligman, noted author, University of Pennsylvania professor, and founder of Positive Psychology, said, "The way in which we describe to ourselves why positive or negative events happen is known as our 'explanatory style.'" He was able to categorize the way we explain such events as the three Ps: permanent (does not change), pervasive (always happening), and personal (you have something to do with it).

In his book *Learned Optimism*, Seligman explained that pessimists, essentially, believe that *negative* things that happen are personal, permanent, and pervasive. Optimists view *positive* things that happen the same way—as personal, permanent, and pervasive. And, in both of their "explanatory styles," they foster what they believe.

Ultimately, Seligman concluded that optimists believe that bad events have specific causes, which will pass; while good events will enhance everything and create more opportunities.

It is intriguing to hear psychologists like Herb and Seligman hypothesize about exactly when qualities like pessimism and optimism become hardwired. Are we born with these proclivities? Do we develop them by the age of two? Five? Ten? Wherever the fine line is drawn, they all agree that by the time we are adults, those qualities are predominantly stable. These inherent personality traits are expressed through our thoughts, feelings, and actions.

While heredity and circumstances can predispose us to approximately 60 percent of the traits we possess, Sonja Lyubomirsky, a professor of psychology at the University of California, Riverside, argues that we can affect the remaining 40 percent of how we express our traits through how we act and think. That potential resides in all of us. As Katharine Hepburn's character declares to Humphrey Bogart's in *The African Queen*, "Nature, Mr. Allnut, is what we are put in this world to rise above!" How we act and think is where our intentions can make all the difference in the world. And how we can tip the scales, enhancing our optimism.

As Lyubomirsky underscores, "Being optimistic involves a choice about how you see the world." It does not mean denying the negative or avoiding all unfavorable information or constantly trying to control situations. What it does mean is realizing that optimistic outcomes are dependent upon our efforts."

Herb explains, "Ultimately, what we are all seeking is to be realistically optimistic." This involves hoping for and working toward desired outcomes, while focusing on opportunities that increase the likelihood of our attaining personally meaningful goals.

Realistic optimism is particularly important when we are considering our goals and plans. Do you see such situations as challenges or opportunities?

Such framing can be quite powerful, as it has been shown to influence willingness to take risks, as well as our aspiration levels. That is why, realistically, having a positive attitude is likely to pay off.

At the end of the day, for some people, it does not matter if the glass is half empty or half full, so long as you or someone you know can help you fill the glass.

Questions to Ask Yourself About Being Optimistic

These questions are posed for you to consider as you create your own vision, tap into your personal strengths, and pursue your own leadership journey. Your answers to these questions will help you understand how optimism factors into your approach to leadership. You are encouraged to consider these questions at different times, as your answers will undoubtedly evolve and change as your leadership journey unfolds.

1. When do you feel you are at your very best?
2. How could you create more of those experiences?
3. When things do not go your way, what is your first thought?
4. How much control do you believe you have over negative events?
5. How much control do you believe you have over positive events?
6. Do negative events upset you more than positive events please you?
7. Do you believe that most people are optimistic or pessimistic?
8. Do you consider yourself mostly optimistic, mostly pessimistic, or somewhere in between?
9. Do you surround yourself with people who are mostly optimistic or mostly pessimistic?
10. What makes you smile?

Looking Far and Wide

It was around that time that word of Caliper's approach to assessing talent started to spread across the Atlantic Ocean. Herb and David were asked to speak on a whirlwind tour of eight British cities by the Institute of Marketing.

For several reasons, this seemed to be a perfect introduction to possibly taking their new approach to assessing talent into another country. First and foremost, of course, there was no language barrier. And while there were certainly cultural differences, it was assumed that they would not be as vast and significant as might be found by starting in, say, Japan or China.

Still, there would be cultural differences that would be intriguing to explore. It was like taking what they had learned about the qualities that distinguish top-performing salespeople back into the laboratory. Would there be similarities between the best salespeople in the United States and in the United Kingdom? Would there be cultural differences between salespeople in London, Edinburgh, Belfast, and Cardiff? Or, would those differences be more a matter of style than substance?

"It was a very exciting time," Herb recalls. "I remember sitting on a Boeing 707 with a publicist we brought over for the occasion, and he kept marveling, 'We're going where Shakespeare lived.' He just couldn't get over the notion that we were flying to the place where the Bard came from." It was a time of new awakenings and infinite possibilities.

Herb adds, "We were most intrigued by exploring the differences and similarities between top-performing salespeople on each side of the pond, as they say over there."

However, when Herb was interviewed by journalists in the United Kingdom and started presenting at some of the seminars that had been arranged by the British Institute of Marketing, he realized that something was not quite clicking. His enthusiastic message about the qualities that distinguish top-performing salespeople was not hitting the right notes. Something was clearly off.

It did not take him long to figure out that in the United Kingdom, the profession of sales doesn't have anywhere near the same status as it does in the United States.

"In the United States, while salespeople are certainly the brunt of many jokes, and salespeople may be perceived as being overbearing or over-the-top by some people, there is still a clear understanding and appreciation that 'nothing happens until something is sold,'" Herb says.

He adds, "That's why, in the United States, there is only one option for fast trackers who are looking to make more money than their peers, are seeking increased responsibility, and are too impatient to slowly climb their way up the corporate ladder—sales."

"But in the United Kingdom," Herb says, "they do not even like the word *salespeople*. Someone who was 'selling' would rather call themselves a 'relationship manager' or an 'account consultant.'"

So the first thing that Herb learned, as he began traveling internationally to introduce his concept of assessing potential and talent, was how to adjust his presentations in order to connect with his audiences in different countries and cultures.

"What became clear to us quickly," he says, "is that executives in other countries are not looking for some American expert to come along and tell them how to do things better. That approach would backfire very quickly."

He learned that while executives in other countries were intrigued by new and evolving innovations from America, he needed to partner with executives who were already established and respected in those particular marketplaces. That became a winning combination for introducing Caliper's approach to hiring top talent in new countries. "They wanted to hear what we had to say," Herb says. "They were very intrigued. Absolutely. But when it came to us delivering our hiring approach in other countries, we needed the credentials and credibility of someone who was already on the ground, and an integral part of that country. Ideal partners for us were consulting companies who were already succeeding in a tangential practice to ours—such as sales or leadership training. Then they could introduce our approach to the clients with whom they were already working. And we could introduce them to our clients who were expanding into their country. That, we discovered, created the ideal synergy," he says. He discovered that the ideal partnership had as much to do with strategy as it did with chemistry. These new partners would bring insights, knowledge, credentials, and expertise to a marketplace where they already had an established presence, which ideally positioned them to introduce Caliper's new, more precise way to assess and develop talent.

Over the course of the next several decades, Caliper would learn to refine that approach to different marketplaces. Offices in Canada, Mexico, and the United Kingdom were soon opened. With the success of those ventures, offices were opened in Australia, Brazil, China, France, Germany, Japan, Singapore, Spain, and Sweden.

"What continually fascinates me," Herb says, "is that each market has unique differences and similarities. We are constantly tweaking as we learn about some of the subtle differences that distinguish us all and some of the universal truths we all share in common."

Herb shares that sometimes he has decided to enter growing markets because there is a clear need to help companies assess the potential and talent of individuals. More often than not, though, he says, "Caliper has developed capabilities within certain countries because our key clients, such as Kohler, were looking to expand into those countries, and they wanted to bring us along with them. They were looking for our expertise to help them identify and develop talent in those new and emerging marketplaces. In such cases," Herb adds, "your clients often lead you in directions and to places that you would have never imagined. In order to service large, multinational companies, we had to become global in our own capabilities. As a result, our in-depth personality assessment is now available in over 20 languages."

What has he learned that impresses him most about why people succeed in different cultures?

"When all is said and done, there are more similarities than differences between people in Boston and Paris, just as there are between people from Philadelphia and Madrid and between people in Manhattan and Billings, Montana. What is inside of someone may be expressed differently because of cultural differences. Some of us may be more subtle, while others are more boisterous. But inside of people, where it really matters, we have found there is the same distribution of qualities driving us including empathy, resilience, need to persuade, assertiveness, conscientiousness, etcetera. It is just a matter of measuring what is inside of someone, then realizing that it will be expressed differently in different cultures. So, someone who is driven to persuade others may express that drive differently in Japan than they would in England.

But the drive, that need to persuade, will be just the same in both individuals."

Early on, we were asked to help assess salespeople in Tokyo, and we were very hesitant. But, we quickly learned that while there are certainly differences in the approach to selling in every country and culture, the motivation is fundamental and consistent."

Herb adds, "At the end of the day, we are all more similar than we are different." Pausing, he muses, "Sometimes when I hear about all the conflicts in different parts of the world today, I wish we could just concentrate on what we share in common, rather than the differences that we sometimes believe separate us."

What was one of the most interesting findings he has come across as he has entered new countries with different languages and distinct cultures?

"We were very enthused about entering the Czech Republic in the early 1990s when they ceased being a communist state with a centrally planned economy. From our perspective, this was a pure laboratory. As the country embraced capitalism, jobs were being created for which no one had experience. So we were measuring the potential and the inner drive of adults who had never had such jobs. Would they have leadership, management, sales, and customer service potential that had been lying dormant up to this point in their lives? We couldn't wait to start assessing job applicants under such circumstances. The country was trying to find its way. Opportunities seemed to be everywhere. And everyone was trying to figure out how they might fit in.

"Most interestingly," he adds, "as we tested for sales positions, we found that 25 percent of the population had sales potential. They were driven to persuade. What is so incredible about that, to me, is that there was not even the word *salesperson* in the language. Neither the word nor the profession existed before. Yet still, in the newly formed Czech Republic, we found there was exactly the same percentage of the population that was driven to persuade that we have found in every other country in which we have worked. This, to me, was *astounding*. It underscored that there is the same amount of potential—to lead, to manage, to sell, to deliver customer service—everywhere, regardless of age, gender, or culture. None of those superficialities matter. All that matters is that we help to identify the potential of individuals and help them develop their potential to their fullest capability."

How are leaders discovering the talent they need in different countries around the world?

Stephen Inman, director of corporate human resources at Kohler Company, who has incorporated Caliper's assessment and consulting into his firm's hiring and development practices in China, India, France, and England, told us that working in different countries has given him an enormous appreciation and insight into people—and into himself.

Echoing Herb's philosophy, Stephen underscores, "When people ask for my advice about working in different countries, I always tell them to look for the similarities. Don't get hung up on the differences. They have a job; you have a job. They have a family; you have a family. They have aging parents; you have aging parents. They have a mortgage; you have a mortgage. If you look for the cultural differences too soon, you'll stumble on them and highlight them and be confused by them. Instead, look to what you share in common, which is often enormous. If you focus on the similarities, they will trust you. Then they will share with you what the cultural differences are, so that you can appreciate them—rather than have them separate you."

As Stephen considers whether someone has the potential to succeed in different countries, what does he look for?

"I want to know if they are adaptable, flexible, open, and curious. Can they listen well and reflect on what they are hearing? I also want to know if they are skeptical while being empathic. I know that might sound funny, but they've got to have enough skepticism to ask what somebody means when they say, 'It's different here.' They need to probe, to make sure that they understand. But they also need to have enough empathy to listen to someone and not just focus on what they are *saying*, but to truly seek out what is *meant* by the difference."

What do some people possess that allows them to succeed in a new marketplace? Why are some people truly global citizens?

Herb says, "Ultimately, people who succeed in various and diverse situations are willing to take risks. Moving out of a comfortable space can have risks. And if, for whatever reason, you don't take those risks, you can stay within the space you know and not venture forth. Some people are more comfortable leveraging their knowledge and capabilities in their current network. Others are driven by new experiences, new challenges, and new opportunities. It really comes down to how people are wired.

"To succeed in today's global marketplace," Herb adds, "leaders need to be bright and strategic. They need to enjoy developing plans, then be comfortable adjusting them on the fly. They also need to be able to convey ideas and initiatives in a forthright manner, be persuasive, and be equally inclined to listen to ideas from others. The ideal global leader also needs to be flexible, highly organized, and driven to succeed. Setbacks will have to be perceived as nothing but learning experiences. Competing in the global marketplace calls for an ideal blend of the qualities that distinguish top-performing leaders—at hyper speed."

How does Herb decide when the time is right to enter a new marketplace?

"That's when a quality I have, which people are constantly teasing me about, comes into play. I have an enormous amount of urgency.

Essentially, that's a need to get things done *now*. We have a scale on which we measure the amount of urgency someone possesses. Essentially, it goes from zero to 100. And people tease me that mine is in the 200 range," he says. "The truth of the matter is that I just can't sit around and wait for something to happen. To me, that's just a royal waste of time. So, *I'd rather try something and make a mistake than not try something and never know what I was missing.* Sure, I'll listen to all the analysis that anyone on my team can provide me with. Sure, I'll talk with anyone we're considering partnering with and trust my instincts. But when push comes to shove, it is about trying something—giving something a shot, with all you've got. That's the only way to tell whether something will work or not."

That sense of urgency, a defining quality for Herb, brings us back to the beginning of how Caliper started to become international. The speaking engagements and media interviews throughout Britain, arranged by the Institute of Marketing, were going exceedingly well. At every turn, there was extreme interest in everything they were saying. Things were clicking in ways they had never possibly imagined. In the thrall of the moment, David knocked on Herb's hotel door and told him he had a surprise for him. With childlike glee, he led him to the elevator, through the hotel lobby, and onto the street, where he excitedly said, "Run your hands across this." Going along with him, Herb said, "That's nice. What is it?" David said, "It's a 1933 Rolls-Royce convertible. And it is yours." Not waiting for a response, David quickly added, "Behind it is a 1948 Bentley, which is now mine." Herb just started laughing. Then they both were cracking up. Herb finally was able to say, "How did you buy these? We don't have enough money for these." "Not yet," is all David said, still laughing. "But we will." To this day, Herb says, "I don't know how he did it, but he did. We ended up taking them back to the United States and selling them, coming out a little ahead in the deal. But I can say that once, for a very short period of time, I owned a Rolls-Royce convertible."

Psychological Insights—Urgency

"As it turns out," Herb reflects, "one of my main faults might also be one of my major virtues. This fault, if you want to call it that, goes back to when I was a teenager trying to get a date, and it has followed me throughout my personal life and professional career. There is just something in me that cannot wait. If someone says, 'I'll call you back,' I hate it because I always feel that they're not going to call me back."

Is that right?

"Absolutely," he says, definitively. "I find waiting to be worse than anything. It's just the worst part. So, if I'm waiting for a callback, I will, maybe precipitously, maybe too quickly, say, 'to hell with it,' and I will pick up the phone and start dialing. Sometimes that may be a mistake on my part. I may be perceived as being too aggressive or too impatient. But I would rather push the situation forward than sit around and wait, twiddling my thumbs."

As Herb exemplifies, someone with a great deal of inner urgency needs to get something, make that everything, done "right now." Later is too late. Such individuals need to keep moving. And they need that movement to be quick. They find delays to be extremely frustrating. Typically, they cannot stand long deliberations over a subject. Instead, they are motivated to act and keep acting until a successful outcome is achieved.

At the other end of the spectrum, individuals with very little inner urgency will come across as being entirely too laid-back, complacent, and even passive. What's the rush? Tomorrow's another day.

This is not meant to completely dismiss patience as a virtue. There are certainly times, after you have done everything you can, when patience becomes the wisest course of action. And sometimes wisdom prevails.

"It is important to point out, however, that inner urgency can sometimes be confused with impatience," Herb explained. "The difference is that individuals with inner urgency will act to obtain immediate results; whereas individuals who are simply impatient may be bothered by delay, but not necessarily do anything about the situation. Anyone, for example, may feel terribly impatient while experiencing an inordinately long wait in a doctor's office, but an individual with inner urgency is likely to walk over to the receptionist and say that it is impossible to continue waiting, and instead either get taken earlier or reschedule the appointment."

Mere impatience does not denote action. Inner urgency, for good or ill, most often leads to action.

Laurie Dalton, chief human resources officer at gategroup, North America, the world's largest independent provider of catering services for the transportation industry, tells us, "One of the most important distinctions for people who succeed with us is a bias toward action. And, in my view, this is not something you can learn."

By the time somebody is old enough to apply for a job, they either have it or they don't.

Laurie adds, "If you think about it, we are servicing airlines, and a key focus for them is to be there on time. So, we need for our employees to have that quality, so that we can come through for our clients."

Let me just close with a brief memory about Herb. I was in his office one day, and he was outlining three new projects he wanted me to work on. A few minutes later, as I got up to leave, he asked me if the first project was done yet. "Now that's a classic Herb Greenberg moment," I said. He just laughed, adding, "I'm going to hear about this one, aren't I?" "Absolutely," I replied. "Some day I'm even going to write about it in a book."

Questions to Ask Yourself About Urgency

These questions are posed for you to consider as you create your own vision, tap into your personal strengths, and pursue your own leadership journey. Your answers to these questions will help you understand how your sense of urgency factors into your approach to leadership. You are encouraged to consider these questions at different times, as your answers will undoubtedly evolve and change as your leadership journey unfolds.

1. What, from your perspective, is so important that it cannot wait?
2. How do you set your priorities?
3. Are *important* and *urgent* the same for you?
4. How many things in your life are important *and* urgent?
5. If you are constantly working on projects that are urgent, what happens to the ones that are important?
6. What is the most important thing that has ever happened to you? Did you plan it? Or did it just come about?
7. Is there something you did that you would have done differently if you had taken more time to consider?
8. Is there something you wish you had done, but did not do because you decided to wait just a bit too long?

Seeing Inside and Out

As the decade of the 1960s blended into the 1970s, Herb and David decided to go their separate ways. Herb says, "I can't say, for sure, why. Were we too similar? Spending too much time together? Getting in each other's ways? Tripping over each other? Who knows? I think back on it often and wonder if there might have been something I could have done differently. I can't help but wonder how Caliper might have been different if David had stayed. But for whatever reasons, we decided that he would go his way and I would go mine. We agreed that I would buy him out, and Caliper carried on from there."

Now, as a solo entrepreneur, Herb realized he had to look at his business from a new perspective. He and his wife Beverly had also decided to go their separate ways. So now the business became Herb's singular focus.

What was the biggest challenge you had in those early years?

"Money."

Money?

"Not having enough money. Always wondering where the next dollar would come from. So it was difficult trying to spread the word about who we were and what we could do to help executives identify people who would help their businesses thrive. We couldn't advertise. We just didn't have that kind of budget. So we had to grow through referrals— one referral at a time, which was a very slow, hard way to grow. That was our biggest problem—how to get the word out and let executives know what we could do for them," Herb says.

How could he market without a budget?

As he shared ideas and confided with his clients who were leaders in the automotive, real estate, and insurance industries, a lightbulb went on. They all belonged to professional associations where they met to float new ideas, share best practices, and lobby Congress.

How could he become part of that inner circle?

At that point, Herb asked some of his key clients, like Jack Pohanka, who had been president of the National Automobile Dealers Association, to introduce him to the executives who ran the day-to-day operations of their associations.

Through sharing conversations about their mutual needs, Herb was able to create a unique arrangement with the National Automobile Dealers Association, the marketing arm of the National Real Estate Association, and the Independent Insurance Agents and Brokers of America in which they would endorse Caliper's services.

"Being an endorsed member service provided us with marketing opportunities unlike any we had before," Herb says. "Through this arrangement, I was able to speak at their conventions, write articles for and advertise in their publications, and gain introductions to their inner circle. In exchange, Caliper would give the associations' members a special price and return to the associations a royalty on the revenue that their members generated."

For a company with a very slim marketing budget, it was a gem of an idea.

"One of my fondest early memories of speaking at a professional association meeting was sharing the platform with John DeLorean," Herb recalls. "He was already an icon in the industry, having introduced the Pontiac GTO, the Firebird, and the Grand Prix. With his long sideburns, unbuttoned shirts, and jet-setting lifestyle, he was a real nonconformist in the automotive industry."

"I remember that both DeLorean and I gave presentations at an annual automotive conference in the early 1970s that fell on deaf ears," Herb adds. "He spoke with bravado, and quite a bit of profanity, about how the automotive industry had to come up with better ideas for building cars besides just how much chrome to put on the back tail, because the Japanese automakers were going to take away the whole market from them. This was at the time when the oil crisis was just starting to hit. But American automakers thought it would pass quickly and get back to the way things were. He warned them that they had to create cars that did not (and he used the phrase) 'piss away' as much gas, and they needed to do it quickly. Otherwise, he warned them that in a very short period of time, everyone in the room would be doing something besides selling automobiles."

Realizing that he was speaking to an audience that desperately needed to be shaken out of their complacency, Herb recalls, "I told this all-male audience that they were looking for salespeople in all the wrong places. I told them that our studies proved that women could sell just as effectively as men. And if they opened themselves up to that possibility, they could find that within a year some of their top-performing salespeople would be women. Then, shortly afterward, they would find that some of their best sales managers would also be women. And before the decade was out, I added, there will be women owning automobile dealerships."

How did that message go over?

"Like a lead balloon," Herb says. "They were polite, but you could almost hear the good old boys saying, 'Yeah, yeah, yeah, professor. That's really funny."

Still, Herb was learning along the way some of the most important keys to packaging his service. First, and foremost, he had learned to sense an opportunity. The next step was to create a solution that was easily explained and made sense upon reflection, but for which you still needed a specialist to guide you. He had also learned to blend his academic credentials with the demeanor of an executive to become an expert in his field. And, like DeLorean, he was learning the importance of being, at least slightly, provocative. Herb was also learning to have a good time while he was at it.

The marketing model of being endorsed by professional and trade associations quickly took off, becoming largely responsible for Caliper's growth during this period. What evolved were unusually close ties and connections with the associations and their members. As Paul Buse, president of the Independent Insurance Agents and Brokers of America's for-profit operation, said, "We have enjoyed a 30-year business relationship with Caliper that has yielded both financial benefits and positive results for thousands of our independent agency members. 'Do you Caliper?' should be a familiar question to our members nationwide." After several years, Caliper was endorsed by more than two dozen associations, ranging from radio and television advertising to electronics to equipment dealers to healthcare professionals and every profession in between.

Reflecting on how Caliper grew through the strength of the association endorsements, Herb says, "I get a lot of ideas. Some of them are cockamamie. But some of them have helped make Caliper what it is today. The important thing is that I act on my ideas."

During this time Herb married his second wife, Jeanne, who had been working at Caliper for several years. He was attracted by her intellectual curiosity, as well as her sophisticated aura. She quickly became much more integral to running the business, as Herb's partner. Caliper's office, meanwhile, moved from Manhattan to Princeton, where they were renting space in Research Park. Shortly afterward, their daughter Holly was born. At that point, Herb and Jeanne moved to their first of what would be two exclusive homes in Princeton.

As the company continued to grow, they were also able to afford an apartment in Fort Lauderdale, as well as a summer home along the New Jersey Shore on Long Beach Island. They also traveled extensively, often combining business with pleasure.

Herb's sister Zena recalls their mother, whom she describes as being "always nervous about the future," as constantly "worrying about Herb and his business, shaking her head and saying 'I don't know. It's going to all fall apart. He's not going to have any money.' And every time we would see Herb and his family, my husband would say, 'How come your mother is always saying that? And he keeps getting richer and richer. Why is she so afraid?'"

Herb smiles and says, "My mother was always concerned because she didn't think there was any security in this business. She felt it could all go away as quickly as it appeared. Losing her family in the Holocaust clearly had an enormous impact on her. She was always worried and concerned. She felt that if I had pursued the track of becoming a tenured professor, that would have been a much safer and more secure route for me to have traveled."

Growing Up with a Budding Entrepreneur

Throughout their childhood, Herb's sister Linda says that their father could always get a job because he was a very talented cobbler, who could not just repair but also make shoes. But it seemed like he would always get dissatisfied with his employers or, at the least, think that he could do much better. "He was a custom shoe maker," Linda says, "and he could create orthotics and take a mold of someone's foot and create a custom shoe that would fit them perfectly. So he would work for other people. Then he'd try going into business on his own. But he would not know how to price the shoes he created. He didn't have any kind of business sense. Our mother did. And if he had let her take care of the business end, he would have been a rich man."

"That's why we were poor," Herb's sister Zena adds. She remembers being nine years old when her father asked her to deliver a pair of custom shoes he had created for one of his customers. She recalled taking the subway and getting off near the customer's apartment on Central Park South. "And I go into this magnificent building with a doorman, and I never knew that a place like that existed. When I came back and told my mother, she said, 'Yeah, but you know what? Your father hasn't raised his prices like all the other people in his business. The price of leather just went up, but your father didn't feel right raising his prices. So he only charged two dollars for what you just delivered.'" She pauses, then says, "That's why he never had money."

"He never had money," Herb confirmed.

One of the main differences between what Herb's life had become and where he came from was that Herb was willing to take a risk.

"He was always a leader of the pack," Zena explains. "He would just come up with these ideas, decide he was going to do them, and somehow he got everybody to do what he wanted to do."

"He had sheer determination," Linda agrees.

"That, and nothing defeated him. He was not going to fail, period. It was written. He was just determined to get what he wanted, and he always did," Zena says, then adds, "Of course, what he really wanted to do was teach in universities," which is what his parents and sisters all assumed he would do. "It's such a far cry from what he ended up doing," she adds.

Reflecting upon why Herb succeeded as an entrepreneur, Linda says, "You've got to be a bit of a gambler," to which Zena quickly adds, "which we're not."

Even when Herb was a child, his sisters saw in him the spirit and drive of an entrepreneur and, equally important, the willingness to take a risk, to go for it, to give whatever he was pursuing everything he had.

What was it like growing up with a brother who was blind?

Zena says her parents told her that the reason she was born a year after Herb lost his sight was "so that when they were no longer on this earth Linda would not be responsible for Herb alone."

Did that feel like a heavy burden for you, as a young child?

"A lot of people, when they hear that, say, 'Oh, you must feel terrible.' But I don't," Zena says. "It's quite the opposite. From my perspective, I was thinking that my mother was so incredible. She thought ahead of time, and she didn't want Linda to bear all the responsibility by herself. They were concerned that Herb wasn't going to be able to do anything in life possibly, and so at least there would be another person who could help."

Linda adds that growing up with a brother who was blind made her feel like she was invisible.

You were invisible?

"He didn't see me," she tries to explain. "And it had a profound influence on me in many ways."

You were not seen, so you felt invisible.

"Right. He didn't see me. I don't now how else to explain it. But that's just something I grew up with, and it stayed with me."

That's powerful.

"That's very powerful," Linda confirms. "A very important thing in my life."

Growing Up with a Father Who Is an Entrepreneur

Herb's daughter Holly, who now lives in San Francisco and has a private practice while she pursues her Ph.D. in psychology, confirms that growing up with a father who is blind inevitably defined much of her childhood. Sometimes, it used to feel as though she was "going through the world feeling a little bit invisible . . . feeling unseen," she says, although she had never heard Herb's sister express that same thought.

What she also needed to determine, she explains, was "Whose eyes am I wearing? What lens am I looking through?" At an early age, she remembers, "I became his eyes; I was reading and cataloging stuff for my dad—from wines to vitamins to record albums. I could alternate between a Chateau Montroche and a Bing Crosby album in a heartbeat," she says, shaking her head and laughing to herself. She would read to him, and also categorize his collections so he could find what he was looking for on his own. "I was learning an adult way of looking at the world at a very early age, through being the eyes for my father," she says.

Still, she remembers, "My dad and I had a lot of affection between us. I have a picture of us where I'm about three years old, sprawled out all over him, and he's on the couch, hugging me, with a huge smile." They used to play hide-and-seek, and, she recalls, "it always amazed me that no matter where I hid in the house, he always found me."

One of the dilemmas for a child of an extremely accomplished individual, she adds, is the question, How do you measure up? "Trying to live up to his accomplishments . . ." Holly pauses, then adds, "It is daunting to consider. He set the bar very high. In many ways, there is almost an *unbelievability* about all he has done. It is unfathomable to people." So, as she explains, she needed to develop her own standards for measuring her success.

Most interestingly, Holly observes that to consider himself successful, her father "had to make *himself* seen." Pausing, she reflects, *"He wants to be seen for what he has chosen to accomplish.* And he didn't choose the blindness."

"He wants to be seen for what he has chosen to accomplish," I repeated. "That's a great way of putting it."

Caliper helped him to be seen. That's why he focused so intently on making Caliper successful. "Caliper gives him a liveliness and vitality," Holly says. Like the child of many entrepreneurs, she learned that his business was always his baby.

So, with a new wife and young daughter, Herb found a new way to be an entrepreneur. This was when he started to enjoy the fruits of his labor. Holly remembers, "We used to go to Florida or the Jersey Shore for a week, and he was not on the phone the whole time. He was down the beach. And he and my mom used to take cruises and travel all the time."

For Herb, there were different stages to his being an entrepreneur. When he first started, and for most of that next decade, it was all-consuming, filling his every waking moment, as well as his dreams when he was sleeping. Then when he got married to Jeanne, the business supported their lifestyle, which he had never even dreamed possible before.

The Ingredients of an Entrepreneur

Reflecting on his life as an unexpected entrepreneur and the qualities he had to draw upon in order to succeed, Herb says, "There are certain ingredients that all entrepreneurs share. But it is not a formula. It is not like you can take a half-dozen ingredients, add water, put them in a blender, and out pours an entrepreneur. Still, I believe, we all share certain qualities."

Does it start with being a salesperson?

"Being able to sell your product or service or concept is certainly integral to being an entrepreneur," Herb says, "but then there is something that separates the pure salesperson from the potential entrepreneur. Oftentimes, top salespeople like to go from one sale to the next. *That* is what drives them. The next opportunity. And an entrepreneur certainly needs that in him- or herself or to have a partner who has that. But being an entrepreneur goes beyond the next sale. For an entrepreneur, there is a desire to create something more. To create an entity. Ultimately, it is the desire to have something that is you and that lives in you and after you, that is an extension of you, that goes on. And hopefully, on and on."

It is the desire to leave your mark.

"Exactly. To leave your mark," Herb rolls the phrase over. "That's why, in many ways, Caliper is an extension of me, or an expression of me, might be a better way of putting it. It started out with trying to understand the psychology of a salesperson, and that became psychologically autobiographical. In other words, I was reflecting upon, then describing how *I* sell. Of course, there was solid research behind it. But that was our starting place. Then the way we delivered our service, not just through a written report, but most important with a telephone consultation. That consultation was central to how we delivered our service, and, of course, it was a reflection of how I like to connect with people—one-to-one, individually, in a way that explores not just what is, but what can be."

There really are several kinds of entrepreneurs. You started out as an inventor.

"Right," Herb replies. "We saw an opening, we saw a need to be filled, and invented something that did not exist before to fill that void. In many ways, entrepreneurs are trailblazers. Seeing something that did not exist before. Sometimes what is created is brand-new, something that did not exist previously. As Henry Ford famously said, 'If I had asked my customers what they wanted, they would have said a faster horse.' "

Being an entrepreneur is about being able to see new possibilities.

"Exactly," Herb says. "It may be something that never existed before, like the Wright Brothers. Or it might be seeing something that exists elsewhere, but that a particular country or market does not have. Perhaps you are traveling someplace on your vacation and you notice that they do not have any pizza or bagel shops. Well, there's your opening. If you see a place where something is missing, you don't have to be an inventor to become an entrepreneur. You just need the guts to take a shot and introduce pizza or bagels to an area where they are missing—and where you might like to live. That's a win-win."

Some entrepreneurs are also in it for the long haul, while others want to get in, make a lot of money, and go on to their next venture.

"That's true. It depends on your motivations. Some people, like me, want to create something that is an expression of themselves," Herb says. "Others love the idea of starting something new; but then, when it gets into growing the business beyond the initial phase, they get completely bored with the day-to-day operations. They love the thrill of starting something that did not exist before. So at that point, serial entrepreneurs, as they are called, want to sell their creation to someone who can keep it growing. Then they want to look at a new idea to pursue."

In the beginning, it sounds like you could have gone either way with Caliper. Particularly when you say that you and David would have gladly sold your invention if you were offered a tidy sum.

"That's true," Herb reflects. "Sometimes you may not know what is really driving you as an entrepreneur until you are in it. For instance, Mel and Patricia Ziegler cofounded The Republic of Tea after they sold Banana Republic. They are both artists, very creative, and love making an impact. Their creations come from the heart, from their passions. At Banana Republic, clothing became a catalyst for the imagination. Likewise, The Republic of Tea became the emissary for a way of appreciating life—not rushing around with coffee nerves. After the concept of The Republic of Tea became reality, and it grew to be a certain size, however, they sold it to Ron Rubin, who, as a client of Caliper's, has grown the company to be the leading purveyor of premium teas." Herb adds, "I admire Mel and Patricia for being entrepreneurs who know how to start something and are very comfortable getting out and moving on to their next venture, just as I admire Ron as an entrepreneur who knows how to take an innovative concept and grow it from its initial stage to maturity. They all are entrepreneurs at the top of their game, knowing what they are best at and playing to those strengths."

I cannot help but think that it is very rare for a company to continue with its founder at the helm for over a half century.

"If you look at a list of the names of companies that were started in 1961, the year we did, you will see very few that you recognize today," Herb replies, solemnly.

Did you have a Plan B, if Caliper did not succeed?

"Oh, I always had a Plan B," Herb says.

What was it?

Laughing, he says, "Well, as you know, I'm not much for planning. I'd rather be doing. But I have no doubt that if Caliper did not succeed, I'd come up with some plan—or at least the kernel of an idea that would lead to a plan."

So your plan was that you would come up with a plan?

"Exactly," he says, nodding and smiling at the thought. "When people make five-year plans, that always cracks me up," he adds. "Even a plan for what to do next year. That's so far away, with so many things that can happen between now and then. I have no idea what is going to be going on next year. I might know what I want to do next week. But I'm not even sure what I'd like for lunch today. I know the direction I am taking. But *if I try to plan every step of the way, I am going to miss what is happening all around me—which is where the real opportunities are.*" Pausing, he adds, "I believe in the future. And I believe in asserting whatever influence or control I have to help shape what will happen. But I also believe that if I spend my time trying to plan everything out, I will inevitably miss the real opportunities that are presenting themselves each and every day."

Do You Take Time to Savor?

Do you spend more time anticipating, experiencing, or remembering?

Now in his mid-eighties, when Herb looks back on his leadership journey, he can savor the memories of each step. Even the early hard times are softened because of how his life turned out. While it was occurring, he could savor the opportunities he had to help people who were on welfare find gainful employment and create new opportunities for themselves and their families. Savoring those moments was enhanced because of the disappointments he had earlier when he was trying to help people as a counselor in the Department of Welfare.

But it was not until a decade after he started his company that he could savor at least part of what he was accomplishing *while* it was happening. "It was then that I knew we were succeeding, " he reflects. "In the beginning," he reminds us, "I could not have possibly anticipated that things would have turned out as they did. The most David and I were hoping for was that a large insurance company would buy the assessment we created, and I would go on to become a professor with a very nice size savings account."

Savoring is all about time. It is when time disappears. It is also about before, during, and after. It can be when we are anticipating something positive, intently enjoying the moment, or reminiscing to rekindle former positive feelings. To savor you have to be *in the moment*, free from cares and worries, focused and mindful of all that is possible.

"How can you free yourself to savor your best moments?" Herb asks. "It is a formative question and one that I still struggle with." Our minds can quickly and easily get cluttered with all the little things that can dismay and distract us. How can we take the time to appreciate all that is going well—and allow those experiences to truly uplift us—rather than allowing the world's frequent, harping, little negative occurrences to weigh us down?

Do you get pleasure from looking forward to a positive event? Or do you feel anticipating is just a waste of time? Can you fully appreciate good things? Or do you find it hard to hang on to a good feeling? Do you enjoy looking back on happy times? Or is reminiscing disappointing for you?

How you answer these questions can say a lot about how much you allow yourself to savor, and whether you may be prone to savor the moment, or anticipate something positive, or reminisce about better times, according to Fred Bryant, professor of social psychology at Loyola University.

In savoring, we are allowing ourselves to bask, give thanks, marvel, or luxuriate in positive experiences—something with which many of us could use help. All too often, we may just find ourselves running from one activity to another, as if chasing our own tails. Herb says, "But even when something marvelous happens, do we take the time to *enjoy*? It is often easier to say that than it is to do. Still, it is so important to be able to roll past the less consequential negative aspects of life and focus more on those moments that go so well."

Whenever I think of savoring, I am reminded of the Nicolas Cage character in the movie *City of Angels* when he asks Meg Ryan's character to describe what a pear tastes like. He says, "Describe it. Like Hemingway." And she says, "You don't know what a pear tastes like?" To which he responds, "I don't know what a pear tastes like to *you*." Then she looks at him, and says, "Sweet. Juicy. Soft on your tongue. Grainy. Like sugary sand that dissolves in your mouth. *How's that?*" And he says, "It's *perfect*."

Do you allow yourself to take pride in your accomplishments (basking)? Can you become sensually absorbed in the pleasure of an experience (luxuriating)? Can you experience and express gratitude (thanksgiving)? Are you able to lose yourself in the wonder of a sunset (marveling)?

As you reflect on these questions, keep in mind that *our beliefs are the lens through which we see the world*. They are the glasses we put on in the morning, which provide the patterns we see. As we become more self-aware, we can identify our patterns, and then, to the extent we desire, change our lenses.

Psychological Insights—Entrepreneur

Several years ago, I was with Herb when we were presenting to a class of students at the University of Michigan who were in their final semester of getting their masters of business administration. The course was on entrepreneurism. About half the students were taking the course because they wanted to be entrepreneurs. The other students were taking it because it interested them, but they had intentions of pursuing a corporate career. All of the students had taken Caliper's proprietary in-depth personality assessment, the Caliper Profile, and Herb was going to share the composite results with the class, highlighting some of their key qualities, while sharing with them some of his personal experiences in starting and running his own company. After the introductions, Herb said, "The only thing I can tell you, with absolute certainty, is that one person in this class is *not* cut out to be an entrepreneur." As they all leaned in, he explained, "The reason I know this is because you were each offered to take Caliper's in-depth personality assessment for free—and one of you did *not* take the assessment. What I can tell you, for sure, is that I never met an entrepreneur who passed up an opportunity to get anything for free."

As the class laughed, he added, "I will tell you about how I succeeded, and some of my lessons along the way. But what I really want to tell you about are some of my failures." At this point, everyone was really leaning in. Everyone in this class was already highly accomplished. Just to be accepted into this exclusive program, they all had impeccable grades, and most had very impressive experiences. They were all straight-A students. Very few had gotten a B+, let alone an A– in anything. And here was a successful entrepreneur talking with them about his failures. It was like a breath of fresh air as Herb talked with them about buying a radio station and losing a lot of money on it, as well as the seven times he was fired before he went into business on his own. He was giving them permission to fail, so long as they were willing to pick themselves back up, brush themselves off, figure out what they had learned, and go on, even more determined. Avoid perfection, he told them. Trying to be perfect is the enemy of success.

Before telling them about some of the best (and worst) times he had while creating and growing Caliper, he told them how he had lost over $2 million when he bought a minor league basketball team called the Trenton Shooting Stars. "The kid in me was thrilled," he told them, "because I had selected a manager and players who went on to just miss the championship by one point. But the adult in me could not make the venture profitable. I was not able to fill the stands with spectators. In retrospect, a lot of it had to do with Trenton being in the middle of a saturated marketplace for basketball—halfway between New York and Philadelphia, with rabid NBA fans in both places, while also being surrounded by college teams such as Princeton and Rutgers, who have their own strong fan bases. So the kid in me succeeded, while the adult lost a ton of money."

Then he speculated that it is very interesting that when you meet and interview entrepreneurs, you often discover that they readily admit to having been lousy employees. "Some of them, like me, got fired. More than once." That is not to say that being a lousy employee means you will automatically be a successful entrepreneur. But there seems to be a pattern going in the other direction. Entrepreneurs are, generally speaking, not adept at following the rules of others. They need to create their own rules—if not their own mayhem.

Another "must have" for an entrepreneur, according to Herb, is an inner sense of urgency, a need to get things done *now*. "Entrepreneurs don't have the patience to hear, 'I'll have to take that up with the committee,' or 'Let me mull that over and get back to you.' They like to end each meeting knowing that something is being moved forward."

Entrepreneurs are also "unwilling to be molded by external pressures, such as going along with a plan because 'this is the way things have always been done' or making decisions based on what the majority wants to do even though his or her heart is saying that the course of action is absolutely wrong," Herb explained.

"They would also prefer to control, rather than to be controlled," he added. It's about rules. On the one hand, not liking them, but at the same time, wanting to make them your own.

As Herb quickly added, though, "this is not a formula or a recipe for an entrepreneur." Those same ingredients could backfire. You might just wind up with someone who has been fired a number of times, tends to aggressively rail against prevailing wisdom, is a bit of a control freak, and is always storming ahead, starting new projects without thinking them through.

Or, you might end up with a visionary entrepreneur.

Entrepreneurs are the ones who surprise us. They're the ones who can take things to the next level.

The one ingredient that they all share is a willingness to take risks. "Entrepreneurs know that they could be making a huge mistake with each and every move," Herb said. But they also know that they could be making a bigger mistake by not making a move. Standing still is not an option when everything is moving around you. *You have to be willing to take a risk, to lose, knowing that with each loss, something is gained.* And that next shot might take you to a whole new level of success.

There is also a strong competitive spirit—a desire to win, to achieve goals, to surpass what they and others have done before.

In addition, there is a need to latch on to something about which they can feel passionate; something that impels them forward and to places they would not go otherwise.

On a final note, there is also a strong desire to make an impact. They want to hear the sound of cymbals crashing. "They want to create something that is bigger than themselves, and that is meaningful," Herb said. "They want to influence, if not change, the world around them."

Questions to Ask Yourself About Being an Entrepreneur

These questions are posed for you to consider as you create your own vision, tap into your personal strengths, and pursue your own leadership journey. Your answers to these questions will help you consider whether being an entrepreneur is part of your leadership journey. You are encouraged to consider these questions at different times, as your answers will undoubtedly evolve and change as your leadership journey unfolds.

1. Under what circumstances do you wish you were more assertive?
2. With what people do you wish you were more assertive?
3. How could you assert yourself in such a situation so that it became a positive affirmation for you and everyone else concerned?
4. What is so important to you that you are likely to take a risk on making it happen? Why do you want to do it?
5. What is your risk tolerance? Would you take a risk if you were 90 percent sure of the outcome? Would you do it if you were 75 percent sure of how things would turn out? What about a 50-50 shot? Would you do it if you only had a 10 percent chance of the outcome turning out as you wished?
6. How often do you question others?
7. How often do you question yourself?

Sports

In the early 1980s, Herb asked his neighbor, architect Bob Hillier, to design and build offices for Caliper in Princeton on Mt. Lucas Road. Everything was looking up. The consulting firm was growing at levels that afforded Herb opportunities to experiment in ways he never could before.

One of those attempts was to purchase an AM radio station, which was floundering at the bottom of the local marketplace, and try to convert it into a station that would remind him of what radio used to be like when he was a child. He wanted to create a radio station that would eloquently and memorably engage people, the way Edward R. Murrow used to enlighten his audience about politics and Red Barber could make his listeners feel like they were actually at the baseball stadium.

"I was able to identify and bring on talent for the station," Herb says, "and we were able to produce very good content, including interviews with dignitaries like President Carter on several occasions. But the engineering problems became a royal nightmare. This was something that I knew too little about. We were wasting money left and right trying to fix the signal. We had a lot of fun with the formatting. We had shows on folk music, jazz, and even some old-time radio shows, featuring Jack Benny, Jimmy Durante, and Fanny Brice. We even brought in some of the soap operas, like *Jack Armstrong, the All-American Boy*, and *Captain Midnight*. We had our listeners on the air and very involved. And we had plenty of commercial time, but the only way we were compensated was in gift certificates—for restaurants, hot air balloon rides, even cruises. But very little actual money. So, after a few years, I licked my wounds, cut my losses, and sold the station." Pausing, he adds, "Radio has always been an important part of my life. It was not just a way to get information, it was like school to me, where I learned the art of storytelling from some of the finest on-air personalities there ever were. So, while the radio station didn't turn out like I hoped it would, I'm glad I gave it a shot."

Selling the radio station freed Herb's imagination to pursue other ventures. As a child, besides radio, one of his most significant passions, of course, was sports. Being in the dugout with the Dodgers was formative in his childhood, if not transformative. He loved listening to and analyzing games. And he was constantly intrigued by why some players made it in the major leagues, while others, who seemed to have all the talent in the world, fizzled out. Then the wheels started to spin. This is where his love of sports and his expertise as a psychologist merged in a dreamlike way.

Herb got the notion that the assessment approach he had developed to hire top-performing leaders, managers, salespeople, and customer service representatives could also be adapted to picking draft choices for professional sports teams.

"I started with the assumption that virtually all players seriously considered by scouts and coaches have a great deal of talent. Yet the vast majority are not able to take their game to the next level," Herb says. They don't live up to their scholarships in college or their signing bonuses in the major leagues. So talent alone was not the predictor of success. "The fact that a player dominates in college because of talent simply does not mean that he or she could dominate on the professional level when going up against people of equal and better talent," he adds.

Herb started experimenting with the Rutgers football team, where he still had some connections. He says, "This was a dream come true. We were learning a lot about why some athletes who were all-stars in high school could not take their talent to the next level. We also learned why some athletes could surpass others with equal talent. Ultimately, what matters is what is in an athlete's heart and what is in his or her head."

After refining his theories and seeing them come to fruition at the college level, a few years later, Herb was in Nantucket with Gordon Gund, a co-owner of a professional basketball and hockey team—the Cleveland Cavaliers and the (then) Minnesota North Stars. "We were on his boat, sipping a wonderful white wine while looking for clams. As the conversation unfolded, Gordon asked if I thought I could help him with his draft choices for the North Stars. I told him that I didn't know the first thing about hockey, but I could help him pick players who were competitive, self-disciplined, and believed in themselves. Gordon said, 'You're on.' And that's how we started in professional sports.

"After I helped him select some players who went on to be very successful, the team moved from being a doormat to a competitor," Herb says. "Gordon then asked if I could help with his basketball team, and I was thrilled, because that was a sport I knew. In fact, I graduated from City College the year they won the NCAA and the NIT tournaments—the only team ever to have achieved that success. With Gordon's confidence and insights from the general manager, Harry Weltman, we worked together to help take the Cavaliers from a losing team into one that became highly competitive. Then, when Harry moved on to manage the New Jersey Nets, we continued to consult with him on his draft choices. That led to us working with several dozen professional basketball, baseball, and football teams, including the Orlando Magic, the Philadelphia Eagles, the Chicago White Sox, and the Chicago Cubs."

What qualities distinguish top performers?

"If what the scout sees on the field was enough to go with, there would be no mistakes in the draft: every pick would be successful. What they can't see is what is inside the player. There are three essential qualities needed for an athlete to live up to his or her potential," Herb says. "That's what we study. Are they self-disciplined, competitive, and do they have a positive sense of their self? Those three qualities have to be lined up for a player to actualize his or her potential."

Just as he started off his work on successful salespeople with two, then three essential qualities, Herb had created a model for superior athletes that could be simplified into three indispensable, but interdependent, attributes. With them, in substantial amounts, an athlete might be ready for the next level of competition. Without them, success was highly unlikely.

"We started with *competiveness*," Herb says. "Competitiveness is obviously the starting place for anyone who succeeds in sports, and that same competitive drive we have found is one of the distinguishing qualities of a great leader in business. Defined succinctly, competiveness is that burning need to win with all of your heart and soul. It's not just the desire to win the game, which every athlete has, but it is also having the instinct to compete with every move you make on the field or the court. For instance, if someone comes dribbling the ball down the court, you want to block him or her, stop him or her, get the ball out of his or her hands—whatever you need to do to win that play. Every play is equally important to a top performer."

We know that competition brings out the best in top performers—in sports and in business. Ultimately, records are only broken in the heat of an important competition. Nobody gives their best performance when he or she is in training. Training just gets athletes ready for the arena.

"If an athlete has a strong competitive drive, it has to be backed with an equally strong sense of *self-discipline*," Herb adds. You cannot stay at the top if you are not comfortable in high-stress situations. Succeeding at that level comes from being ready, being prepared. To succeed when the pressure is on, you have to be inner-focused, self-directed, and self-disciplined.

"In essence, self-discipline is that internal taskmaster—that voice inside of a top performer that says, 'I want to practice because it will make me better.' It is self-discipline that distinguishes an athlete who comes to camp in better shape than last season from an athlete who arrives overweight. To truly understand the competitive nature of an athlete or a business leader, it is critical to understand the important difference between self-discipline and external discipline. Self-discipline comes from within, who someone is. External discipline is simply understanding what *they* want you to do—or the 'should system.' In Freudian terms, self-discipline is the ego, while external discipline is the superego," Herb explains.

The third quality shared by top-performing athletes, as well as the best leaders, is *resilience*. "All top performers must know how to face rejection and even failure if they want to succeed. *The ability to move beyond life's inevitable rejections will determine success much better than talent alone,*" Herb says. "In baseball, a Hall of Fame hitter might bat .333 over his career. That means that for every three times he comes up to bat, two of those times he does not get a hit. He fails two out of every three attempts. To keep going, to come up to bat the next time, after not getting on twice in a row, a potential Hall of Fame hitter needs to believe that *this time is his time.*"

Herb adds, "We often hear about the phenom in baseball—the hot rookie who comes to camp batting .400 or striking out everybody in sight. Everything seems golden. Then he encounters an inevitable slump—and does not know how to get out of it. He starts changing his swing, holding the bat differently, but nothing works, and within a few months, he's out of the game, never to be heard from again," Herb pauses, then adds, "From a Freudian perspective, this ties into whether the athlete accepts the slump as a confirmation that he or she is really not good enough, or whether his or her ego is able to bounce back from the slump, and see the next opportunity as a fresh start."

Herb says, "The athlete who personifies resilience for me is Muggsy Bogues, whom we both got to meet and write about in our book *Succeed on Your Own Terms*. Everything about him just resonates resilience." To this day, Muggsy remains the shortest NBA player of all time. All five feet, three inches of him. Muggsy saw basketball as his way out of the ghetto, where he said, "The difference between Muggsy Bogues, NBA player, and Muggsy Bogues, dead body, is so small. It scares me just to think about it." He saw basketball as his ticket out, his way of getting a scholarship to play college ball, then to get to the pros. So when his name got called as a first-round draft pick, he said, "I heard them say that the Washington Bullets had selected Tyrone Muggsy Bogues. That was it. All the naysayers telling me I would never make it. All the folks saying, 'He's too small.' And here it is. I'm walking up there to accept my hat and shake Mr. Stern's hand. You know. Five feet, three inches. I'll tell you, that was just amazing. The whole universe was just lifted off my shoulders. It was like, 'Hey, you finally made it. You're here! Your time has come!' "

Herb reflects, "Muggsy is a guy who knows where rejection belongs," and that attitude helped him overcome the most unbelievable odds. From the time he started playing basketball on lots in Baltimore's projects through high school, college, and the NBA, Muggsy said what drove him was that he always wanted to prove that the people saying he was too small were wrong. In one sense, Muggsy said, "It was in one ear and out the other. But it hurt. So in another sense it was just another measuring stick as far as proving them wrong. And then it gets to the point where it's even more important than just proving them wrong."

One of the keys to his success was that, as Muggsy said, he could "use negative emotions as internal motivation."

When Muggsy meets young people, he likes to tell them, "We all encounter a lot of negativity through life. But my life proves that anyone can overcome negativity. You can do anything you want to do in life if you have a fierce belief in yourself, a strong will, a big heart, and some role models to inspire you."

Herb adds, "As with athletes, leaders in business are bound to experience slumps and rejections, no matter how determined they are. There are going to be times when they are not going to want to face another possibility of rejection. To move beyond those feelings of vulnerability and rejection, athletes and leaders need a solid sense of self-esteem."

Depending on the position, Herb notes, he will also look for other attributes in an athlete, contingent upon the team and the position for which an athlete is being considered. But the starting (and in some cases, the stopping) place is whether an athlete possesses competitiveness, self-discipline, and resilience.

With that model, Herb got the introduction for which he had been longing. Here is how Joe McIlvaine, who was then the general manager of the New York Mets, describes it. "I always have questions," he says. "And one of my favorites is to ask athletes who are successful at the major league level, 'What percentage of your success do you attribute to pure talent, and what percentage is psychological?' And I've never had a top player say that less than 75 percent is psychological. More often than not, they say, it is closer to 90 percent. That question to me is so important because I've seen so many players who ended up being flashes in the pan, they just wash out once the competition gets better, and they suddenly retreat, go home, and they're done."

Joe adds, "So I was looking for someone like Herb to open the door to what was going on inside the heart and mind of each of these players. When Herb told me he could tell me about their self-confidence, their mental toughness, and their ability to control their emotions on and off the field, I was interested, but skeptical. While he was recommended to me, I still needed to see how deep the insights were that he could provide."

Herb recalls, "I agreed to assess five of players on the team, whom Joe said he was having some problems with. I shared with him what I believed to be going on with four of the players, including one who I said might be a bit explosive at times, even have a tendency toward violence. Joe said, 'You're right. He actually attacked another player last week.' But then I told him that I couldn't find anything unsettling about the fifth player. In fact, he seems like someone who will give it his all and play up to every ounce of his potential. Joe just laughed and said, 'You're right on that one also. I just threw him in to test you.' That player, unbeknownst to me, was Tim Bogar, who played for the Mets for three years, then the Astros, then the Dodgers before going on to be a coach and manager at the professional level."

So Herb was brought on to advise the Mets on their draft choices. The Mets, who came as close to the Brooklyn Dodgers as a team possibly could. While it was not quite like revenge, the Mets, at least, were the crosstown rivals to the New York Yankees. And that's all that mattered.

Joe says, "As the manager, you're always trying to put the odds in your favor. And my feeling was with Herb, the odds were certainly in our favor. He was a psychological advisor, just as our scouts were talent advisors. Then, by putting all that information together, my job was to predict what a 17- or 18-year-old kid would be like five years from now. So, we are trying to predict the future."

Studies showed that the athletes Herb was able to recommend for the Mets (and other baseball teams) were getting twice as many hits as those he was not recommending. The ones he recommended also had at least twice as many home runs, scores, and stolen bases. In basketball, the results were similar. The players Herb recommended had almost three times as many points per season, with at least twice as many rebounds, blocked shots, assists, and steals.

One of the main lessons for leaders is that if you want to surround yourself with top performers, you need to create a culture that encourages and rewards top performance. Many leaders mistakenly believe that top performers will inspire and raise the level of performance of everyone else around them. "But we have found this is not what happens. And it is, in fact, the opposite of what top performers are looking for. One thing we've learned about top performers, in sports and in business, is that they want to be connected with *other* top performers," Herb says. "They do not want to be working side by side with someone who will fumble their pass or not complete their part of an important project on time." Your top performers do not want to be working with people from the junior varsity team. They want to be surrounded with people who will make them stretch and be their best.

Herb adds, "Some of the most innovative companies we are working with are creating situations in which their elite performers push one another to levels they would never reach if they were working with less-accomplished colleagues. We are working with these innovative companies to have their star performers working side by side on major initiatives. That's what engages top performers. They want to be part of a winning team and make a real difference."

That is why learning about what drives champion athletes and the best leaders is so vital. Competitiveness, self-discipline, and resilience. These three characteristics are essential to succeeding in sports and in business.

"Where do these qualities come from?" Herb asks. "Deep inside." What really happens psychologically to a professional athlete is that their competitiveness, self-discipline, and resilience kick into high gear so that they can succeed when it is game time. On a psychological level, they know that they need to dig in and turn up the volume on those three qualities in order to succeed. And, like all of us, they have an inner need to succeed—because in that success, they feel that they are being themselves at their very best.

As a leader, the only thing we can tell you for certain is that if you surround yourself with people who *do not* possess these three qualities—then the top of your game will be somewhere in the middle.

Knowing Where Competition Belongs

Herb and I learned a lot about competition when we interviewed Geoff Bodine, who is one of NASCAR's 50 greatest drivers of all time. Together, he and Dale Earnhardt Sr. made NASCAR a contact sport in the late 1980s and early 1990s. They had characters loosely based on their antics in the film *Days of Thunder*, starring Tom Cruise.

If you google the name Geoff Bodine, among the top hits will be YouTube videos of a major crash he was involved in at the Daytona Speedway. It is considered the worst crash in NASCAR history. That's quite a thing to be known for. It occurred on February 18, 2000. Geoff's vehicle hit the wall going nearly 200 miles an hour. Cartwheeling down the track in flames, his vehicle disintegrated into a fiery heap. The top of his vehicle was sheared off, as the engine rolled down the straightaway, and pieces flew into the stands. The vehicle's metal disintegrated until all that was left was a roll cage—before it was hit again. And again. And again. Even in slow motion, you cannot tell how many times his vehicle flips over and over and over.

Two months after that accident, Geoff was behind the wheel, driving 200 miles an hour again. He says the NASCAR officials wouldn't allow it now, but he was able to fake them back then. If he moved his head too quickly up and down or to the right or left, things got blurry. (And if you've ever driven in one of those simulators, you know that driving at that speed is all about your peripheral vision. What is coming behind you and next to you can mean the difference between winning and crashing.)

What was driving him?

He says, "I'm just competitive."

There was something else. What was it?

He paused, then says, "I didn't want to be replaced."

That was his fear. That's what drove him. That was an essential part of what made him so competitive.

"Look, if you're off the circuit for two months, they'll find somebody to take your place," Geoff quickly adds. "So, yeah, you're in a hurry to get back in that seat so nobody else gets in it. That's the real fear for race drivers. That's why we'll drive even when we're hurt. We do that a lot. I've done it throughout my whole career. Just about every race driver can tell you, 'Yeah, I've driven with a broken this or a torn that.' We drive hurt all the time."

Geoff, who says he is now able to look inside himself more honestly, told us that the same competitive spirit that made him one of NASCAR's top drivers of all time also ruined many of his personal relationships—because he didn't know how to keep his competitive drive where it belonged. He didn't know how to keep it on the track.

How Self-Discipline Can Transform an Outcome

"As you reflect on self-discipline," Herb says, "ask yourself if the people you surround yourself with have willpower and strength of mind."

When you make important decisions together, do they drive those ideas and those projects to completion? Or are you constantly monitoring progress? Do too many things somehow fall through the cracks?

If you find yourself checking up on progress too much—and being disappointed with the results—then you're not leading, you're pushing.

Do the key players in your organization drive themselves? Or are you pushing them?

If you're pushing too much, well, you know the story about the guy who pushes the rock up the hill all day long, then starts his next day pushing the same rock up the same hill.

Are you spending too much time looking back to make sure that what you thought was supposed to get done is completed?

"If so, the people you're surrounding yourself with are not providing you with the support and the freedom you need to look forward," Herb says.

As a leader, you have to make sure that those key individuals you surround yourself with have the self-motivation, the willpower, the strength of mind, and the drive to come through. That quality starts with an inner need to come through for themselves. Make sure you are surrounding yourself with people who are self-disciplined. Otherwise, your job will be less about leading and more about cleaning up.

The Difference Between Competing in Sports and in Business

Many executives are drawn to watching professional sports. Part of the reason is undoubtedly because they thrive on competition. Which sport you prefer can also say a lot about you. Do you follow rugby or tennis? Are you into aggressive team sports with few rules or individual sports that test an athlete's endurance?

That is probably why so many sports analogies find their way into business settings: "The deal was a slam dunk." "We need a new game plan." "That was a home run." "We need to put on a full court press." "We'd better punt." "We really need a Hail Mary pass here."

The legendary quarterback Roger Staubach led the Dallas Cowboys to two Super Bowl victories and became a client of Caliper's after he founded The Staubach Company, an enormously successful real estate enterprise. Roger has a clear perspective on sports analogies. When we asked him which sports analogies make the most sense to him in the corporate world, Roger told us, "Competition is certainly important. Being clear about your goals is crucial. But for me, the key to developing successful organizations is all about team building. It's all about the people you surround yourself with. Succeeding in business, in sports, and in your life is a matter of pulling together people you can trust, who are honest, who have their priorities in line, who have the talent, ambition, and desire to reach beyond themselves and make something really big happen—particularly when the pressure is on."

Roger's thoughts are profound in their straightforward simplicity. This, after all, is from the guy who personified grace under pressure, and who every Minnesota Vikings fan can tell you threw the "Hail Mary pass," then coined the phrase.

In many ways, though, winning in professional sports can be a lot easier than winning in business.

For starters, in sports, you can see who you are competing with. You are eye to eye with them on the same playing field. You are there together, and you have a chance to physically confront them.

You can also watch tapes of how they played against other teams, and rewind the tapes as you analyze the team's strengths and weaknesses and strategize your game plan. Professional sporting events also last for a specific duration—for example, four quarters or nine innings. There are time-outs. There are clearly defined and agreed-upon rules and boundaries. And there are referees or umpires to take care of disputes.

The competition in business, however, does not play that way. In business, all bets are off. Your competition is no longer in your neighborhood. Your competitors can be on the other side of the world. They can be awake when you are asleep. They can come from anywhere, at any time, and from any direction, when you least expect it.

Psychological Insights—Competitiveness

"By their very nature, top performers, whether in sports or a business setting, are competitive," Herb says. "They want—make that *need*—to win. It is in every fiber of their being. The best are always competing. No question."

He adds, "But I want to provide just one cautionary note about people who are always competing. The question that needs to be asked is: Who are you competing with? Yourself or someone else?

"The answer matters" he advises. "There are times when you absolutely have to face the competition head-on. And you want to come out on top. Then there is another type of competition that comes from within. These people compete with themselves. They are continually trying to improve. It's part of who they are. As a leader, it is important to have a perspective and understanding of both sides of the competitive spirit. You may need to rally the troops to compete against a competitor or other forces in the marketplace. Then you want to surround yourself with talented individuals who are constantly challenging themselves to improve. Having that competitive spirit within your organization, you can beat any foes."

Herb pauses, then adds, "Steve Jobs was particularly effective at finding that balance between the two. On the one hand, in his iconic 1984 advertisement, which he ran only once during a Super Bowl game, he was telling his employees and his customers that they were standing fiercely against the conformism that IBM then stood for. Later, Jobs turned his sights on Microsoft." For Jobs, there was always a nemesis to focus on—and against which to define his company as David righteously standing up against the dim-witted Goliath. On the other hand, he was also able to inspire and challenge those *inside* of his organization to constantly create, innovate, and improve *themselves*. That understanding of what it means to be competitive—against your competition, while also competing with yourself—is a winning combination.

"I just want to caution," Herb adds, "there is just one thing you want to make sure of. If your people are constantly competing with others, rather than themselves, that energy can be turned against your own organization. We have been brought in to consult with organizations where some top performers were competing with others on their own team—rather than with the competition. That can be extremely destructive."

Among a leader's most important responsibilities is to make sure that the executives on his or her executive team are collaborating with each other—rather than competing with each other for the limelight. That internal competitiveness will sap your energy, waste valuable time, and create an environment where the only movement will be backward.

Competition, when it is turned inside an organization rather than focused at the marketplace, becomes very destructive. "We have seen it literally destroy organizations," Herb underscores.

Leaders need to create an environment where disagreements can be discussed openly—where there is the understanding that inside of a healthy debate is where the best solutions arise. Only inside of such collaboration is where true innovation will occur.

Herb adds, "This does not (in any way, shape, or form) mean that leaders should look to surround themselves with 'yes' people. What they should be looking for is positive people. I feel strongly about that. People who are very negative upset me. They ruin group dynamics. They second-guess everything. And they can ruin any momentum you are trying to achieve. Our job, as leaders, is to be realistic, yet instill optimism. That's the only way to inspire others and create opportunities."

It is vital for leaders to harness the competitive spirit within their organizations—and focus that competitive spirit on their competition. Only then can our competitive drive to continually improve be unleashed in a focused way, propelling us to new heights.

Questions to Ask Yourself About Being Competitive

These questions are posed for you to consider as you create your own vision, tap into your personal strengths, and pursue your own leadership journey. Your answers to these questions will help you consider how competitiveness factors into your leadership journey. You are encouraged to consider these questions at different times, as your answers will undoubtedly evolve and change as your leadership journey unfolds.

1. Do you continually drive yourself to improve?
2. Who are you really competing with?
3. Are you competing with someone else in an opposing company?
4. Are you competing with someone within your organization?
5. Are you competing with yourself?
6. Are you competing with the shadow of someone who is in the back of your mind?
7. Or are you driven by a sense of obligation to someone else's expectations?
8. Are you constantly competing? Or do you know how to turn it off—particularly in your personal relationships?

New Ways to Lead

In the late 1980s, Herb and his wife Jeanne went their separate ways. After going back in time and dating some of his early flames, Herb met Sunny, whose smile could light up a room, and certainly his life. She, like Herb, had obtained a Ph.D. in psychology from New York University, but from a younger generation of professors. They soon married, then, a few years later, they adopted two children, Alex and Sally.

Reflecting on his two business partnerships that had dissolved, Herb says, "When I was leading the company with David and then with Jeanne, we lived and breathed the business. It was all around the clock. It was constant. There was very little separation between our work and our play. It all seemed to blend."

Were you like bookends—in that you were each bringing distinct talents to the partnership that complemented each other?

"No. David, Jeanne, and I were all very similar. Maybe too similar. We were very driven, assertive, persuasive, and always looking around the corner for the next opportunity," Herb responds. "So, in both partnerships, we ended up doing things together, all the time. Perhaps that became too much. Who knows?" Pausing, Herb adds, "I do think it is doable for a husband and wife to run a business together, but it can be very difficult to separate personal disagreements from business disagreements. They can all seem to blend together. So everything can become merged and magnified. The hard times can be very tough. But, then again, the good times can be wonderful. Eventually, with each of my business partnerships, it got to the point where something that once worked was not working anymore—undoubtedly, for very different reasons."

With a glint in his eye, the entrepreneur in him adds, "Actually there can be a very lucrative consulting practice in helping family businesses ease their way through some of these inherent difficulties."

Now for another entrepreneur who might have acted on his impulses, consulting with family businesses might have led to a new direction for the company. But Herb, as he is quick to say, is not one for planning. He is more for seizing opportunities that present themselves and running with them, as fast and hard as he possibly can.

That is exactly what he did when the next opportunity presented itself, which, like so many things in Herb's life, tied back directly to something he had been pursuing much earlier.

Out of the blue, he got a call from the executive director of Aurora, a London-based organization that advances women in business. She was most interested in coordinating a study with Caliper to see if women leaders in the United Kingdom might be, in some way, different from women leaders in the United States. The idea immediately intrigued Herb. It reconnected him with his dissertation, in which he uncovered the potential of women and others who were not given an equal opportunity, arguing that they deserved a fair break on the strength of their inherent merits. So there was a natural appeal, as it connected with Herb's long-held convictions. What he did not know at the time was that the study would also help to position Caliper on the cutting edge of thought leadership, focusing on how leaders are changing as a result of the world becoming flatter, as Thomas Friedman so succinctly put it.

Herb says, "By looking at women leaders in the United Kingdom and the United States, we initially thought we might come up with some subtle, possibly counterintuitive findings that would prove interesting. Instead, we came up with a study that had enormous implications far beyond that—for how global leaders today need to adapt in order to be effective."

The study included the results of Caliper's in-depth personality assessment, along with comprehensive interviews with women leaders from some of the top companies in the United Kingdom and the United States, including Accenture, Bank of America, Deloitte & Touche, Deutsche Bank, The Economist Group, Enterprise Rent-A-Car, Ernst & Young, IBM, International Paper, Johnson & Johnson, Kohler, Lloyds TSB, Molson Coors, and Morgan Stanley.

"At first, not surprisingly, we did not find any significant differences between the women leaders in the United Kingdom and those in the United States," Herb says. "But as we matched them against a representative sample of leaders from our database of nearly a half century, some surprising differences arose. The aha moment was when we said out loud, 'Of course. Most of the leaders in our database have been *men*.' Now that's when our findings became interesting *and* significant."

The study was published widely and presented at conferences in both countries, leading to further studies and presentations throughout Europe, South America, and Asia. The consistent findings were that women leaders were more empathic and flexible, as well as stronger in interpersonal skills than their male counterparts. "These qualities combine to create a leadership style that is inclusive, open, consensus building, collaborative, and collegial," Herb explains.

As a result, women leaders are showing up differently, which is changing our collective perspective and understanding of what it means to truly lead.

"A story told to us by Sara Mathew, who went on to become chairman of the board of Dun & Bradstreet, particularly impressed me," Herb says. "In many ways, Sara's story demonstrates the key findings of our study. When we asked her about a career-defining moment, she told us about weathering an unexpected storm that tested her very core. Her openness and candor about sharing what happened during one of the biggest mistakes in her career is admirable—and, in my view, the clear sign of a true leader."

Essentially, in a previous position with another Fortune 500 company, Sara decided to completely revamp the firm's investor relations program. Without getting into the details, the introduction of this innovative program fell apart at the seams. She told us, "I did a terrible job, as nearly every major financial publication in the country cited. I could go on and on citing what went wrong. It was years ago, and I can still remember every detail like it was yesterday." Just imagine waking up and having your name on the front page of the *Wall Street Journal*, describing a mistake you had made at work. Ultimately, however, Sara was able to turn the situation around, and the investor relations program she created turned out to be one of the best available. As she told us, what she learned was "the most important time to act is immediately after something goes wrong. It's recognizing the situation and admitting that, yes, I made a colossal mistake." Then she went back and figured out exactly where, when, and how things went awry. She examined how she could have handled the situation differently, what resources she had within the organization and, most important, how to convince her CEO to ignore the media and the stockholders and give her a second chance.

"The qualities she demonstrated—belief in herself and her cause, her disappointment in its failure, her feeling the sting of rejection very personally, her ability to learn from her mistakes, her persuasiveness, her open style of problem solving, her carrying on with a newfound confidence, and her willingness to take risks—are those that helped her win," Herb says. "And they are precisely the unique blend of qualities embodied by women leaders in our ongoing studies."

The study clearly demonstrated that women leaders, first and foremost, are listening differently. And there is the implication that, as a result, they may be hearing things that might otherwise fall through the cracks.

Herb adds, "The strong people skills prominent in women leaders allow them to read situations accurately and take in information from all sides. In that way, women leaders are able to bring others around to their point of view or alter their own point of view, depending upon the circumstances and the information they uncover. Since they are inclined to come at a subject from their audience's perspective, the people they are leading feel more understood, supported, and valued," Herb explains. "The male leaders we've studied, on the other hand, have a tendency to start from their own point of view. This is something they have to be aware of. They have to be careful not to force their perspective and try to convince through the strength of their position—rather than actually persuading. It is important for them to lean in and listen more, rather than just push their point of view."

Susan Webb, executive vice president at JPMorgan Chase & Co., confirmed that, for her, the most important part of convincing someone is to make sure that the person is fully educated on the subject and that he or she understands all the issues and ramifications. "Then, together, I like to think through all the options available to us," she told us. Susan added that she believes persuading is as much about listening as it is about directing. "I want people to be open to different viewpoints, challenge their initial ideas, and to be onboard with a solution that we have arrived at together," she said.

Herb says, "This is a perfect expression of how women leaders, because of their inherent strengths, are able to convey a willingness to listen, to be open to change, and to sense new possibilities."

It is also interesting to note that the women leaders in the study were shown to rebound and learn from setbacks in a way that was somewhat different from their male counterparts. "These women leaders demonstrate a unique approach toward dealing with disappointment, rejection, or situations that don't work out their way," Herb says. "They feel the sting of being set back. They may even dwell on it, and tend to be a little self-critical. But then, as Sara Mathew demonstrated so beautifully, they will muster their assertiveness, shake off any negative feelings, and learn what they need to do to carry on."

Kate Rutherford, a partner at Accenture, confirmed, "With women, it is all about confidence and helping them believe that they can do whatever they want to do. And they do not have to change themselves in order to be successful. I find myself mentoring aspiring women and giving them that push to get over being so hard on themselves."

The study also clearly showed that women are leading teams, solving problems, and making decisions differently than their male counterparts. "The difference in leadership styles between men and women starts with listening," Herb notes. "Not just listening to form your answer, but really listening, learning, reflecting, then implementing a plan that incorporates the best of everyone's ideas."

Lady Susan Rice, managing director of Lloyds Banking Group Scotland, told us, "To learn you have to keep asking. It's all about asking questions. The people I work with will say that the process of my asking them questions helps them clarify their own thinking, and they actually come out a little sharper. That takes a lot of trust. My job, as I see it, is to set a clear strategy, ask the right questions, and encourage our managers to be the experts in their business."

Herb adds, "This inclusive style of leadership that incorporates facts and perspectives from as many sources as possible positions women leaders ideally for the future, as our global economy continues to evolve."

Possibly the most surprising finding in the study was that women leaders are more likely to ignore rules and take risks. Herb says, "One of my favorite explanations for that came from Mara Swan, executive vice president of global strategy and talent for Manpower Group, who told us, 'Women didn't make up all those rules and regulations, so why should we focus on following them?' "

Herb adds, "Women leaders are venturesome and definitely less interested in what 'has been' than in what 'can be.' They will run the risk of occasionally being wrong in order to get things done. And with their fine abstract reasoning skills, they will learn from their mistakes and carry on."

Several of the women pointed to taking on assignments that nobody else on the company's executive team wanted. Then, by succeeding in those high-profile situations, it helped to catapult their careers. That is particularly worthy advice for anyone looking to advance his or her career.

Herb concludes, "These personality qualities combine to create a paradigm of leadership that is ideally suited to today's workplace, where information is shared freely, collaboration is vital, and teamwork distinguishes the best companies."

Your Style of Leading

"One of the distinguishing characteristics of great, enduring organizations is that they put a lot of thought into the development of leadership," says Jim Collins, the coauthor of the acclaimed *Built to Last: Successful Habits of Visionary Companies.*

But this leads to an interesting dilemma for companies.

Because, as Warren Bennis, a pioneer in leadership studies, famously said, "Managers do things right, while leaders do the right things."

If managing people and leading an organization draw upon different strengths, then how can potential leaders rise through the ranks of management? If managers succeed by maintaining the status quo, they run the risk of just blending into the woodwork, and their leadership skills will remain hidden, unrecognized, and undeveloped. However, if they rock the boat, other managers may feel threatened and try to subvert them.

"The ultimate question for leaders is: How can you identify and develop someone who has the potential to replace you—realizing, of course, that the future may call upon them to be very different from you," Herb says.

This brings forth a huge and daunting question for leaders:

How can organizations break out of this cycle to truly identify and develop the promise of future leaders?

"It starts with having a very clear and focused strategy for recognizing, developing, and rewarding those who show real leadership potential," Herb says. "For a leader, you always have to have your eye down the road, as you look to where your organization can go, and which people can help take it there."

He adds, "Leadership is not something that you can designate or anoint. Leadership is about the willingness of individuals to step up, take responsibility, become accountable, accept risk, and move forward. When you see someone who has those qualities and the drive to continually improve, then, with recognition, mentoring, training, and experience, they might evolve from managing to leading." He adds, "But there is no simple formula."

Part of the dilemma is the enormous difference between managing and leading. Learning how to lead is becoming comfortable with the unknown. "When we are managing a project, we want to know all of the variables so that we can be assured of the outcome," Herb says. "When we are leading, we are often dealing with the unknown. We have to become comfortable holding two seemingly contradictory thoughts in our heads at the same time. Then we need to be able to find a way to lead through that ambiguity. As leaders, we have to be comfortable with our own doubt, then realize that we don't need to have all the right answers immediately, all the time. But we do have to keep asking. And coming up with the right questions: for ourselves and for others. Then we need to know when it is time to stop deliberating and act."

Herb pauses, then adds, "Leading is also about how you deal with mistakes—because they will happen on your watch. No doubt. So leading means being open and honest enough to take responsibility when a mistake occurs on your watch, apologize out loud, learn from it, and carry on with a fierce determination in a new direction."

What else does a leader absolutely need?

While it might sound funny to say out loud, a leader needs followers. Otherwise, a leader is someone just marching around by him- or herself, possibly going off into the sunset, or, perhaps, over a cliff.

"In order to inspire followers, a leader needs to have a clear vision," Herb says. "Ideally, this vision needs to have emerged from the core of his or her life. When others sense that core belief and see you expressing it confidently and enthusiastically, *then* they will be willing to sign up, to be part of a mission that you and they believe in. After all, why would someone follow you if they did not know where you were going?

"That's why history has taught us that while autocratic leaders might be successful for a very short while, democratic leaders are the ones that have changed the world," Herb adds.

People will follow a leader if they believe in him or her—and if they believe in where they are being led. They also want to know that their leader believes in them. Loyalty is a two-way street. The strongest leaders express *and* reflect genuine concern for those with whom they surround themselves.

While, at first blush, that might sound simple and obvious, *how many leaders have a clear sense of not just the strengths and potential, but also the aspirations and dreams of the people with whom they are working?* How many have even just had a conversation where they have asked those they are working with what they really love about what they are doing? And what they would change, if they could?

"Such conversations can be so brief, but also so transformative," Herb says. "By way of a quick example, one of our clients told me that he had two customer service people working for him who seemed just out of sorts. One of them was handling travel, and he could tell that she was not enjoying it the way she had previously. The other was dealing with customer complaints, and he could tell that her nerves were starting to fray. As he talked with them about what was going on, he came to realize that the one who was dealing with customer complaints actually loved travel. She enjoyed going to new places and talking about new experiences. The other person was a homebody. Everyone called her Mom. She was always getting people to open up, then helping them solve their problems. All he had to do was listen to them, then put two and two together and switch their jobs. And he said, 'Now they both love what they are doing.' It was as simple as that." As simple as showing the people around you that you truly care and that you're there for them.

But how do leaders create an environment where people feel comfortable saying what they love and hate about their current jobs? How many leaders openly ask questions about the aspirations and dreams of everyone on their team?

"Being able to open up the lines of communication is extremely important," Herb emphasizes. "It is not just about being heard. Leading starts with listening." As leaders, we need to be able to communicate in a way that is compelling when we are addressing a large audience, as well as personal when we are connecting with someone individually. That is a rare talent, combining an uncommon set of abilities.

He adds, "Leading is also about being able to inspire others and succeeding through *them*, as you help them succeed."

Just consider that back when Herb received funding from the United States Department of Labor and the National Alliance of

Business to help people move from welfare to the workplace, he had to relocate his offices and increase his number of employees from a dozen to just shy of 100. It is one thing to be able to have a vision and convey it convincingly. It is quite another to pull it off, to seize an opportunity and create a way to manage the outcome—through the people that he hired and the teams he developed.

So, in addition to having a vision, which they are able to convey compellingly, leaders also need to be able to look down the road and sense changes in the environment that will require them to alter their course. "The best leaders we have worked with are able to see the big picture, as well as to sense changes in the marketplace, competitive threats, technological advances, or economic shifts to which they need to respond—often on a dime," Herb underscores.

It takes an unusually keen and flexible mind to be able to create a new path for your organization (which, of course, you become attached to), then to realize that you have to alter or completely change your newly devised plan in order to get around the next bend. It takes keeping your mind very open. Otherwise, it can be too easy to simply cull out the information you are perceiving in such a way that it confirms your mindset, your preexisting sense of reality.

When all is said and done, leadership takes a complex mix of competencies, including having a vision, communicating in a clear and motivating way, being driven to achieve results, sensing the need for change, managing innovation, developing teams, coaching individuals, delegating and empowering others, objectively and effectively managing the business, and succession planning. "Very few of us, regardless of how talented we may be, are equally effective at all of those key responsibilities," Herb is quick to say. "We just have to keep stretching." Keep stretching, so that you can always be "just a little better."

"Becoming an effective leader is a process," Herb says. "I don't think you are endowed by the universe to be a smart, effective, intuitive leader. I think that if you are inclined to be a leader, you have to give it a shot. Go for it. That means putting in your dues, learning from your mistakes, and maturing into the leader you were meant to be. It is like Malcolm Gladwell talks about it taking 10,000 hours for a musician, an athlete, or a leader to become an expert and stand out from the crowd. Then, once there is enough ability, the thing that distinguishes one performer from another is how hard and smart he or she works." As Gladwell notes, "That's it. And what's more, the people at the very top don't work just harder or even much harder than everyone else. They work much, *much* harder."

While the best leaders share certain qualities, when all is said and done, becoming a leader is an individual journey—combining drive, will, determination, talent, opportunity, and just a dash of good fortune.

Lessons from Our Worst Bosses

Recently, Herb and I asked a room full of nearly 100 first-time managers who were attending a seminar we were conducting, "How many of you have had a manager who was so wonderful that he or she became a mentor to you?"

We were knocked out when most of them raised their hands.

"You are among the fortunate ones," Herb told them. (Ordinarily, when we ask a room full of first-time managers that question, less than half of them raise their hands.)

Then Herb asked, "What did you learn from your mentor that you carry with you and you bring to your approach to management today?"

We heard enthusiastic stories about mentors who brought people under their wings, who confided in them, who shared their thought processes on difficult decisions, who included them in high-level meetings, and who honestly cared about them and their future.

Then, I asked, "How many of you have had a manager who was a complete jerk—someone who you swore you would never be like?"

(I've always believed that any good question reversed is an equally good question.)

And everyone raised their hands.

So, I pursued, "What did you learn from that lousy manager that you carry with you today? Because of their dreadful example, what have you promised yourself you will never be like as a manager?"

The answers did not surprise us. Some said they were treated shabbily. Others said they were pumped for ideas that were then repackaged and presented as the awful manager's ideas. Others said their lousy boss was demanding and moody. And others said their horrendous manager would blame things on everyone on their team.

Herb says, "What did surprise us, though, was the energy in the room." People inadvertently interrupted each other, then apologized, as they excitedly wanted to share their story about what their jerk of a boss had done.

As the room became clamorous, Herb and I thanked them and told them that they were helping us discover something quite amazing.

Ironically, we sometimes learn more from people whom we do *not* want to be like, from the jerks of the world, than we do from those who have our best interests in mind.

Or maybe it's not that we learn more from them. Maybe it's just that we remember them more and still feel the passion of wanting *not* to be like them. If we ever become leaders, we promise ourselves, we will be the exact opposite of them.

The last thing in this world that we would want is for anyone, in any way, to even vaguely confuse *us* with *them*.

So we carry their negative messages with us. Deep inside. We embed them in our subconscious. And we insist, with every fiber of our body, we swear that we will not be like them.

So, here's to all the jerks we've had as bosses. And to all they taught us about ourselves.

Thank you, you absolute jerks!

Your Leadership Strength Test

A true measure of leadership is what we call *The Strength Test*. "This is not a measure of the strength of the leader, but how strong the people are with whom they surround themselves," Herb says.

How much disagreement is there among your leadership team? How much healthy debate? How much open dialogue is there? How many secrets?

"There is a false concept that leaders help keep the boat steady," Herb says. "But I believe that a true reading of how strong a leader is can be measured by how willing he or she is to have their boat rocked from time to time."

Has the leader set a tone where he or she can be questioned? Is collaboration encouraged? Do ideas emerge, morph, and improve? Or is the environment really an echo chamber, where people are encouraged to agree with the prevailing wisdom, keep their heads low, and compromise? How far is someone allowed to go with his or her curiosity? Or is there an unwritten rule that the leadership team is there to protect the status quo?

As the Pulitzer-Prize winning historian Doris Kearns Goodwin shared, Abraham Lincoln's political genius emerged after the one-term congressman rose from obscurity to prevail over his better-known rivals to become president.

The differences between Lincoln and his opponents were striking, as they differed over slavery, with feelings so entrenched that secession and civil war seemed inevitable.

"As Goodwin tells us, Lincoln succeeded because of the strength of his convictions and character, as well as because he possessed an extraordinary ability to put himself in the place of other people, to experience what they were feeling, to understand their motives and desires," Herb says.

It was this capacity that enabled Lincoln as president to bring his disgruntled opponents together, create the most unusual cabinet in history, and marshal their talents to the task of preserving the Union and winning the war.

Herb notes, "Ultimately, as Goodwin shares, the new president overcame the obstacles he faced because he understood the potential and talent of his former rivals, brought them into his confidence, listened to them, and won their respect. His ability to recognize divergent points of view and pull them together forged a stronger executive team than had ever existed in the White House and helped shape what we have come to know as one of the most significant presidencies in the nation's history—at a time when we needed it most."

Lincoln's lesson for leaders is to surround yourself with people who are, at least, as strong as you. He also encouraged leaders to:

- Lean in.
- Listen.
- Let those around you know that you value their opinions
- Make them aware that you want to hear their thoughts and feelings—whether they agree with you or not.
- Create the space and time to reflect.

And finally, tap into your integrity and ingenuity, as you blend the best of those voices into your own and create something that is bigger than yourself—bigger than anything you or they could ever have imagined.

Psychological Insights— What Are You Controlling?

Understanding control—what we can control and what we cannot—is vital for leaders. By its nature, control comes with many inherent contradictions, if not ambiguities. "While leaders certainly want to feel that they are able to exert control over the situations they encounter, it is equally important for them to realize that they need to give up some control in order to gain control," Herb says.

While this may, at first, sound like a contradiction, just ask the people in your organization what brings out the best in them. What is their favorite project they have worked on? When did they give it their all? Invariably, you will hear that it was a project in which they had a sense of autonomy, a sense of purpose, a sense that they could make something happen and that they were contributing to something very meaningful and much larger than themselves.

Leaders need to recognize that by being overly controlling, they can squelch the creativity that the people in their organization are seeking to express. "Too much control results in creating an environment that is negative and even toxic," Herb notes.

Control, it turns out, is has a Goldilocks effect. Too much or too little is too bad. Handled inappropriately, without trust and care, control can be a leader's downfall. "What needs to be controlled is the outcome, the quality, the progress," Herb underscores. "I believe that effective leaders do not control others, but they want to control the results." That is a very important distinction. Leaders can easily be confused by that sense of control, and the power that comes with it. Then, they myopically make it all about themselves rather than about what they are trying to achieve.

Consider this to be a fair warning.

Questions to Ask Yourself About Your Style of Leading

These questions are posed for you to consider as you create your own vision, tap into your personal strengths, and pursue your own leadership journey. Your answers to these questions will provide insights into your style of leading. You are encouraged to consider these questions at different times, as your answers will undoubtedly evolve and change as your leadership journey unfolds.

1. What are your top three leadership qualities? How can you enhance those qualities?
2. What quality that is not one of your leadership strengths would you most like to work on developing?
3. What do you believe it takes to be a great leader?
4. Whom do you admire as a leader? Why?
5. What do you believe it will take for you to step into your next (or first) leadership role? How will you know when you are ready?
6. How do you know when someone else is ready to step into a leadership role in your organization? What will you do to prepare him or her?
7. What is the biggest challenge you are facing as a leader?
8. What have you had to give up to be a leader?
9. How do you connect most effectively with the people you are leading?
10. What do you enjoy least about leading?
11. What do you enjoy most about leading?
12. Where do you want to take your leadership potential from here?

Back Against the Wall

Just after the turn of the century, Herb relocated Caliper's headquarters to a space twice the size at 506 Carnegie Center in Princeton. At the time, his consultancy employed over 200 people domestically and half that many in a dozen offices around the world. Caliper's growth had been consistent throughout the previous decade. By helping companies of every size and shape hire top performers, Herb's firm was a bellwether of the economy. As the economy improved, Caliper's position strengthened along with it.

"Everything was looking up," Herb says. "I remember one of our top consultants calling me. It was in September 2008. He was talking so quickly, I had to ask him to slow down, just to make sure I could understand what he was saying. He was just boarding a plane, and he was absolutely ecstatic. It turned out that he had just left a meeting with one of our key clients and had signed a contract for the largest engagement in Caliper's history. It was a yearlong program, with multiple opportunities afterward. I told him I could not wait to see him, hear more about it, celebrate, and start planning our next steps," Herb recalls. "Then, a few hours later, he called me, completely despondent. I've never heard someone's tone change so quickly in such a short period of time. His plane had just landed, and he was reading me an e-mail in which our client said that, because of the financial crisis, all contracts for the coming year were being cancelled."

With the fall of Lehman Brothers, and other investment and commercial banks suffering huge losses, panic spread. "It was like falling off a cliff," Herb says. What began with the bursting of an $8 trillion housing bubble led to a collapse in business investment. As consumer spending and business investment dried up, there were massive job losses. Each day, the news got worse and worse.

In that financial tsunami, we were all knocked for a loop. Some of us had our insides knocked out. Others had our hopes dashed to the ground. All of our dreams were put on hold. The setbacks, for many of us, were devastating. Careers were dashed. Businesses went under. Homes were lost. All of us were in some ways set adrift, left unsure as economic, professional, and personal challenges combined to twist and test our very souls.

As we entered what was to become one of Caliper's most challenging times, Herb asked me to become president of his organization and, together with him, help lead the company through these economic storms. It was a request that I was honored to accept. Together, Herb and I spent our days meeting with our key clients, our top performers, our financial advisors, and our bankers, who were all conveying the direst messages. Then, in the evenings, we strategized around our dwindling options with our executive team, working out various scenarios, depending upon how long the recession might last. Then we would try to get some sleep.

At the time, more than 95 percent of Caliper's revenue was derived from helping companies improve their hiring. But there was absolutely no hiring taking place. None. Anywhere. Instead, the opposite was happening. Our clients had to start letting people go. And we realized that unless something changed quickly, we were going to have to do the same.

"Every time we turned around, it felt like we were getting knocked down," Herb says. "We woke up feeling good about something that happened, and the next thing we knew, we were hit with two negative things. When you have more bad than good coming at you, it tests who you are and what you're made of."

How could we prepare for a future that was so uncertain? Everything we had learned in the past few decades had little to do with what we were going through then.

As Herb and I sat with one of our key clients, a Wall Street financial advisor whose offices overlooked what at the time was still the devastation left from the World Trade Center, we were told that what we were all going through would continue to get much worse for a much longer period of time before it slowly got better. This financial consultant told us that we would be experiencing the most dramatic employment contraction since the Great Depression. And his prediction that the U.S. labor market would lose nearly nine million jobs, with the unemployment rate exceeding 10 percent, unfortunately, turned out to be very accurate.

When we returned to our offices in Princeton, we saw that two of the four floors of the office building across the way from us were being cleared out. At that moment, as we talked about what we needed to do to persevere, I remember Herb's upper lip trembled, ever so slightly, then his jaw immediately became taut and determined. What I came to realize in that moment, in between those fleeting expressions, was a hint of what made Herb so unique. First he was being open, accessible, and vulnerable, then instantly digging in with a penetrating determination that refused to be deterred.

"We knew that we could no longer avoid making some of the most painful decisions that we have ever had to make," Herb says. "In order to get through the eye of this storm, we were going to have to shrink to half our size. Over 100 people who had been working with us would have to be let go, through absolutely no fault of their own." We were going to have to make those very tough decisions, then refocus and redouble our efforts to keep the company moving in the right direction. We knew that we needed to create a new road map for Caliper. Our focus needed to be less on helping our clients hire more effectively, and more on helping them identify employees who had the potential to become top performers, develop programs to help them and their current top performers reach new levels, coach their key executives, and create more effective teams.

In the meantime, however, we had to make some very quick and difficult decisions—about who would stay at Caliper and who would not. To form a basis for our decision, we reflected upon the qualities that had been essential to Caliper from the very beginning. What was it about the organization that we needed to honor and maintain? By being true to those qualities, we believed, we would find the way to our future.

"We came up with four qualities that have always been at the heart of who we have been, who we are, and who we hoped to remain," Herb says. "First of all, we certainly needed people who were bright. But that was not a distinguishing factor, since everyone at Caliper was certainly bright. We would also need everyone to be optimistic. Optimism is essential when you are trying to defy the odds. And that, interestingly, started to become a differentiator, as it was clear that some people possessed a very strong, upbeat, can-do attitude. The third quality we needed were people who were truly collaborative. Again, that became a differentiating factor, as some people absolutely thrived on connecting and cooperating with others, and contributing to something that was bigger than them. And the fourth quality, which also became very telling, was to be versatile. We were most interested in those extremely talented individuals who were also willing to expand beyond their own area of specialty. The more versatile someone was, the more valuable he or she became, as we were moving into a future that was full of uncertainty."

So, with those four qualities—being bright, optimistic, collaborative, and versatile—we had a firm grasp on what had always made Caliper unique, as well as a compass for our future. "As we were about to make some very difficult and painful decisions about which 100 people we had to let go, we wanted to make sure that we were making those determinations in a way that was consistent with our core values and beliefs," Herb says.

"Still, it ripped my heart out," Herb adds, shaking his head at the thought. "It was excruciating. None of them were let go because of anything they did wrong. We had to let them go because we could not pay them." Herb insisted, to the consternation of our bank, that everyone who was let go receive an attractive severance package. In individual conversations, we also let everyone know that we would bring them back, in a heartbeat, as soon as we could, or help them, in any way possible, to find gainful employment elsewhere.

As I led alongside Herb through these terribly difficult times, I learned an enormous amount about him and about myself. I am reminded of the ending of the movie *Starman*, where Jeff Bridges, playing a visitor from another planet who takes on human qualities so he can somehow get the help he needs to return to his home, says to a scientist, "Would you like to know what I have learned that is most beautiful about your species?" Pausing for a moment, he then says, "You are at your very best when things are at their worst."

In difficult times, when we are challenged as we have never been challenged before, we become more of ourselves. The shy become shier. The hiders go into serious hiding. The planners get out their paper and pencils. And the fighters start swinging for all they are worth.

"Such times test who you are," Herb says, "and give you a chance to confirm what you are made of, and what you believe in."

The same day that we had to let go just over half of Caliper's employees, we had to quickly switch gears to engage everyone who was staying with us. As Herb notes, "We needed to connect with them, individually, in teams, and as an organization and share our plans that would get us through these very difficult times together. We let them know that we were all in pain and reeled from the loss of our colleagues who were no longer with us. We conveyed to those who remained how immensely important they were to us. We reminded them that they embodied Caliper's four key qualities—being bright, optimistic, collaborative, and versatile. And finally, we promised them that, together, we would all prevail."

And, together, we did. We made it through. Sure, we had changed. Our company was smaller. We had to become more efficient. And hopefully, along the way we became a little smarter as well. For Herb and me, though, the time between reflecting and acting had almost completely merged.

Throughout those most trying times, Herb helped me understand that the best leaders have to be able to balance two factors—being able to reflect on all the forces we are facing, then acting faster than our competitors.

Herb and I also quickly learned that whenever we emerged from a meeting together, everyone would be gauging the length and genuineness of our smiles. They were looking to us for signs that everything was fine, that no other shoes were dropping, that we were confident and optimistic about the future. Amid daily signs of contradiction and uncertainty, in individual conversations and town hall meetings, everyone at Caliper wanted to know that *we* felt positive about where we were going. As Herb shared with me at the time, "Our optimism has been challenged like never before. But our job as leaders is to be realistic, while instilling optimism. That's the only way to inspire others and create opportunities. Everyone here needs to know that they can believe in us. And they also have to believe that they can help bring about the changes we need to all get through this together."

Being *realistically optimistic*. It is the ultimate challenge in such tumultuous times. If we overestimated how well we were faring, it could lead to dire results. Still, we needed to convey confidence—in ourselves, and in everyone around us. At the same time, we needed to create an environment where everyone at Caliper felt confident and optimistic about the future. "Equally important, we also needed to encourage everyone to share any and all concerns," Herb notes. "If there were any problems, either within our company or with any of our clients, we needed to know them. They might just be unique situations, or they could be pointing toward a trend. We needed to know. We needed ground-level intelligence, and we needed information that was detailed, up-to-date, and unfiltered. Only openness and trust would get us through this together.

"It was vital that we stay in even closer touch with all of our employees than we ever had before," Herb wisely advises. "Silos would separate us. We needed to know what everyone was picking up on— within our organization, with our clients, and with *their* clients." Our antennas were up. Way up. Listening for meaningful signals, positive, negative, or neutral. We let everyone know that any and all informa tion was welcome, because it could be a vital piece of the future we were creating together.

When we consider a leader's job during such tumultuous times, as Ram Charan, noted author and business strategist, says, it starts with "inspiring and motivating people to go beyond their fears and painting a believable future that is waiting after the storm." The other, equally important realm is "the nitty-gritty of doing business successfully in a very tough and unpredictable environment."

For us, opening each and every door of communication was the most direct way to let everyone know that we were in it with them. Being closer than ever before was important: those connections proved to be our salvation—with our employees and with our clients.

"What was important to realize," Herb says, "was that our atten-tion needed to be completely focused on our employees *and* our clients."

He pauses, then adds, "One of the key themes we were hearing from our clients was that they knew that what really distinguished them was their top performers. Everything else, all the products and services they were providing, could all be copied by their competition in a heartbeat. What would get them through this devastating economic downturn was their top performers, those who were inspired to overcome this challenge, those who were open to change, those who could seize new opportunities."

The problem confronting our clients was exactly the same problem we were facing. And it pointed the way to how we could reinvent ourselves, emerging from these troubled times stronger than before.

We were all in the same predicament—our clients and us. We were all facing the same concerns, fears, hopes, and dreams. Our goal, we conveyed to everyone at Caliper *and* to our clients, was to take the same insights and expertise that we had traditionally shared with our clients in their hiring decisions and focus instead on helping them identify, develop, and retain their current top talent.

We were shifting our paradigm. "When all is said and done," Herb notes, "a company's top performers alone are its competitive advantage." We needed to get closer to our clients, letting them know that we understood their concerns, shared their pain, and could help them attain their goals in ways that they had not previously considered.

"For nearly a half century," Herb says, "Caliper had grown very nicely predominantly by helping our clients improve their ability to hire top talent." This crisis, however, forced us to look at ourselves and our clients through a new lens. "Our new goal was to move the dial on developing talent. Rather than having just 5 percent of our resources devoted to and revenue derived from developing talent, we wanted the development of current employees to become an equal, if not greater, part of our consulting capabilities. We had the talent to help our clients with executive coaching, leadership development, team building, and succession planning. The need was clear. It was just a matter of refocusing our attention, repackaging our services, fine-tuning our messages, and redoubling our efforts," Herb notes.

It was a vision for the future, connected inextricably with Caliper's past. Our new strategy grew from the strengths we already possessed. And it worked. "Some of my fondest moments occurred as we were recovering and knew we were in a position to reach out to some of the people we had to let go and invite them back. Many are here now, and others found their ways to other pursuits that they find very fulfilling," Herb reflects. "In addition, for those of us who went through that most challenging time together, bonds were created that are irreplaceable," he adds. "Now, whenever we hear of anyone in need, whether it is a tsunami in Japan, a hurricane in Haiti, or someone we know coming across hard times, Caliper's employees immediately dive into fund-raising activities. But what I love is that they do it by breaking up into two teams and competing to see which team can raise the most funds. Then, of course, Caliper matches those funds. It is a beautiful way for empathy and competitiveness to merge, forming something very meaningful."

Caliper now has as many employees as it did before the Great Recession, with an organization whose foundation is significantly stronger, since it depends much less on the vagaries of hiring trends.

While we were going through those most difficult times, Herb would periodically say to me, "At least we know where the wall is." Then, feeling behind me, I would nod and respond, "It's right here. And our backs are against it."

Sometimes when our backs are up against the wall, we can surprise ourselves with what we are truly capable of. We can push off those walls and discover something deep within ourselves. We just have to make sure we do not create walls within ourselves, or between us and other people. Walls are for scaling. Or for knocking down and crumbling.

"Together," Herb says, "we moved away from the wall, out of the shadow, into the light of day. All it took was our belief, our faith, our confidence, and our trust—in ourselves and in each other."

Who Are You Spending Most of Your Time With?

Who are your top performers? What qualities distinguish them? Do you let them know how important they are to you? Do you know how to hire people who share their same dynamic qualities?

A short while ago, Caliper surveyed over 500 managers and asked them who they spend most of their time with: Top performers? Average performers? Or poor performers?

Nearly half the managers said that they were spending most of their time with their poor performers.

It begs the question: Who *should* you be spending most of your time with?

"Many executives get trapped into spending their days dealing with problems—often caused by less-than-effective employees," Herb says. None of us plan our days this way. It's not like we're driving to work thinking, "I know what I'll do. I'll get in, grab a cup of coffee, and spend my day solving one problem after another—and never get to the things I really need to do." But how often does that happen?

As Herb notes, "If you, as a leader, are spending too much time with poor performers—or trying to resolve problems caused by underachieving employees—you are probably not focused on the future, on what your company can become.

"Don't spend time trying to change people. Spend time hiring and developing more people like your top performers," he adds.

And spend more time *with* your top performers.

One of Caliper's clients, John Beattie, former senior vice president of human resources at GMAC Insurance, told us a very revealing story about recognizing and developing top performers.

He said that one day he got a call from one of his best performers, and she told him that she was quitting.

He was stunned and asked why.

She said, "John, I'm out here all alone. I can't get any of your time. This just doesn't work for me anymore."

There was a half hour between the phone call and the time she got to his office. During that time, John told us, he did a lot of soul-searching. When she arrived, he told her that he understood completely what she was saying. Then he sincerely apologized. He asked if she would stick with them and give him a chance to prove that he could turn the situation around. And fortunately, she did.

John said that was his wake-up call. He immediately began spending much more time with his top performers, and those who have the potential to be his next top performers. Those who are not stepping in, stepping up, and giving it their all would receive very little of his time.

Essentially, his top performers helped him prioritize and manage his time much more effectively.

Take John's advice.

Spend less time with your poor performers and more time with your best employees—because your best employees want to hear from you and they want to be heard. Focus on the people you want to stay—the ones who would make you feel like you'd been kicked in the gut if they left. Your attention will keep them engaged because they will know that they are valued. And they will be much less likely to start looking for greener pastures.

"Spending more time with your top performers will send several messages to your organization," Herb adds. "First, it will affirm your values. It will be a physical reminder to everyone of who and what you value. Second, it will inspire you and keep you energized and enthused. Equally important, you will gain insights into what is really working for your company. And you will have a much clearer understanding of what to look for when it is time to hire your next top performer."

On top of that, as you get to know your top performers even better, you will also grow with them. You will recognize the distinguishing qualities that you all share and that make your organization so special. Your day will be filled with optimism, resilience, empathy,

persuasiveness, perseverance, the capacity to quickly analyze problems, the knack for arriving at solutions, and the ability to connect
with people in very real, deep, and meaningful ways.

"At the end of the day," as Herb says, "your top performers will
help keep you focused on what works—and how to keep making what
works even better."

Psychological Insights—Rising to Challenges

Herb says that he emerged from this global financial crisis
"stronger and more sure of himself and his purpose."
This certainly was not the first adversity he had encountered.
"But persevering through this challenging time, when our
bank had completely lost faith in our ability to stay afloat,
confirmed my core beliefs," Herb says. He stayed true to
himself. But the experience also strengthened his core beliefs
in a fundamental way.

Scholar and author Warren Bennis explains, "The skills
required to conquer adversity and emerge stronger and more
committed than ever are the same ones that make for extraordinary leaders."

In interviews Bennis and some of his colleagues conducted with more than 40 top leaders in business and the
public sector, they found that they were each able to point to
"intense, often traumatic, always unplanned experiences that
had transformed them and had become the source of their
distinctive leadership abilities."

These "crucible experiences," as Bennis calls them, were
trials that forced these executives to reflect deeply within,
questioning their values and assumptions. They emerged with

a clearer sense of purpose and drive but always, fundamentally, defined by that experience that they had endured.

Why do some people emerge from challenges transformed, while others seem to collapse?

Those who are transformed, Bennis notes, possess two primary qualities: the ability to glean a clear perspective on the context of a situation and the hardiness to persevere without losing hope.

What is important to keep in mind, though, is that while the experiences of leaders like Herb can provide valuable lessons, they are not road maps for you. They are not to be imitated. Rather they are to inspire you to search inside yourself for your own answers.

As Bill George, the former chairman and CEO of Medtronic and a professor at Harvard Business School, says, "No one can be authentic by trying to imitate someone else. You can learn from others' experiences, but there is no way you can be successful when you are trying to be like them." His lesson for leaders is that "people trust you when you are genuine and authentic, not a replica of someone else."

Do not think of the leadership stories from others as the road to follow. Rather, think of them as reflections from the moon at night, lighting the way.

Questions to Ask Yourself About Rising to Challenges

These questions are posed for you to consider as you create your own vision, tap into your personal strengths, and pursue your own leadership journey. Your answers to these questions will provide insights into how your attitude about challenges informs your approach to leadership. You are encouraged to consider these questions at different times, as your answers will undoubtedly evolve and change as your leadership journey unfolds.

1. What is one of your most important core beliefs?
2. Have you ever had it tested?
3. Did it change? Or did you?
4. When you are challenged, what is the first thing you do? The second?
5. Who do you turn to for advice when you are challenged?
6. What quality comes out in you when you are challenged?
7. Which quality would you like to see come out in you the next time you are challenged?

The Future

Herb, who is now in his mid-eighties, says he gets calls every week from investment firms who are interested in buying Caliper. "The conversations are always interesting," he says. "At the very least it gives me insights into what investors believe my company is worth. But I am not interested in hanging up my hat. Why would I retire? To pursue what? What could I possibly enjoy more?"

He reflects, "The reality is, if money meant a damn to me, I'd sell Caliper tomorrow. I'd retire very comfortably. My children would be very comfortable. I wouldn't have to work another day of my life. But so what? I would be completely unfulfilled if I did that."

What do you still want to do?

"I want to make Caliper all that it should be," he says. "Mainly, what I want is for Caliper to grow, to be seen, to be appreciated, to make the kind of impact that our philosophy is capable of making." He pauses, then adds, "My hope is that I built something important. I know it is the gold standard. I'd like everyone to know that. That is what I want to focus on in whatever years I have left to work. Those are my hopes and dreams."

Caliper is about your identity.

"Absolutely. No question," he says. "In addition, though, my attitude toward retirement is that when people do stop working, they have a tendency to die soon afterward. They get very old. They retire at, say 65, and they are vigorous. They are at the height of their powers, then they take up golf or whatever, and a couple of years later, you meet them and they're old already. And a couple of years after that, you're at their funeral. I'm convinced (and this is a very important point for me, personally) that *the brain is the most important muscle you have. And you have to exercise it, just like you have to exercise all of your other muscles.* If you don't, it is going to decay. It's that simple, in my view."

You have to keep moving.

"That's my opinion. When you get to my age, there are constant reminders that time is precious. I was just at City College, where I and a few other alumni were honored, and Floyd Lane was sitting next to me. He was part of the City College basketball team that won both the NCAA and the NIT championships. I can remember him flipping the ball to Eddie Warner, who would drive down and score. Well, Floyd is still with us, but Eddie and most of the rest of them are gone."

When you consider that, do you realize that you are one of the lucky ones? Or do you think that it is sad that they're not around anymore?

"Both things, really. I think it puts me in a frame of mind where I'm in even *more* of a hurry to get everything done that I can get done."

I get it. Some people might figure they are going to just slow down and smell the roses, as they say. But you are thinking, "I've got a lot of things that I need to get done."

"Right. That's me," Herb says, then adds, "It's not that I have a specific goal or a checklist. I just want to do a bunch of things that add up to giving back some of what I got. And I got a lot. So I have a lot that I want to give back."

That's a great message. Let me squeeze in one last question: What about the future of Caliper? How are you feeling about your company's future?

"Well, my son Mark is now president, so that brings a great sense of continuity. And we are surrounded by an executive team that has been with us through the hard times and through some of the best times. And, of course, I have no plans of going anywhere. So I am feeling optimistic. Very optimistic."

In the meantime, Herb keeps moving, always searching, continually striving to be "just a little better." Just recently, he was asked to speak on a panel with several other distinguished business leaders at the White House, his life's work was featured in *Fortune* and *Inc.* magazines, New York University just honored him with a Distinguished Alumni Achievement Award, and his alma mater City College honored him with a gala, commemorating his achievements, his philanthropy, and his moxie.

Fighting Illness

For just shy of two years, Herb has been battling cancer, which came upon him, as it all too frequently does, out of the blue.

Do you mind talking about what you're going through right now?

"I don't," Herb says, "particularly if it might help someone else."

How are you feeling?

"Right now, the only time that I feel sick is occasionally when I am trying to eat. This thing has really impacted my appetite," he says.

What is the worst thing about it?

"I've always resented feeling that I can't change things. And this disease could make me feel that way if I let it," he says. "But I won't. Instead, I'm doing everything in my power to fight it. But it is clear that there are things that I cannot control. In other words, if I reach a certain level of being tired, late in the day, I'm not going to fight through it. I'm going to just go home from work an hour or two early, if I need to, then be back the next morning. I'm rolling with it, but I am also determined to beat it."

When you first found out you had cancer, how did it hit you?

"I couldn't believe it. I mean, that's just not me. I was feeling perfectly well, so it just didn't jive with what I felt was going on," he says. "But, first some blood work, then x-rays and MRIs erased any doubts I might have had."

Was it hard to accept that you had cancer?

He pauses, then slowly says, "I accept that I have it. My lack of appetite, my inability to sleep sometimes, the occasional pain, all that physical stuff lets me know that something is going on. And, of course, I have all the medicine to take, which is an added reminder. But I am waging the battle as it needs to be waged. I'm researching whether there are alternative approaches that my doctors are not considering. But I'm not obsessed about it. You know, I'm just mostly annoyed by it."

Was there any point where you wanted to just rant and rave?

"No. Not really," he says. "What good would that do? I'm not really wondering about 'Why me?' I'm just trying to get on the other side of this."

That reminds me of how you described your initial reaction to going blind.

"I actually resent the cancer more than the blindness," he replies, "because the cancer threatens to wipe me out altogether. I don't think it will, but there is that threat. So I resent it a little more." He adds, "What it probably gives me is even more of a sense of urgency than I usually have, if you can imagine such a thing. You know, I want to get everything done in case, at a certain point, I'm not around. I want to make sure that whatever I can provide has been provided."

When you are researching about cancer and treatments, what frame of mind are you able to put yourself in? Because your research is obviously very personal.

"Now you're going to a scary place, trying to get me to describe how I think," Herb says, smiling at the thought. "I just do it the way I do anything. I am not interested in finding separations between traditional and alternative medicine. I just want to know what works. So I'll explore anything and everything."

In many ways, the personal and the professional have always blended for you.

"I know what you're saying," he says. "When you are a leader, and you recognize a threat, something kicks into high gear." He adds, "It's like in 2009 when the Great Recession hit and we sought the best counsel humanly possible, looking for consistency as well as any insights that might hint at a way out of that situation. You just have to keep looking and believing—in yourself and in the world around you."

Besides improving Caliper, is there anything else you feel an urgent need to do?

"I'd like to go on a cruise," he says. "Then I say to myself, wait a minute. Who am I to think about going on a cruise? (I've been on a dozen or more of them.) But how can I possibly be the guy going on a cruise? That image clashes, if you know what I'm saying."

Clashes with what?

"Well, because I'm poor, I'm broke, I have no money. I can buy a girl an ice cream soda for nine cents, and that's about all."

Are you talking about when you were growing up?

"I'm reflecting," he says. "When I feel sick, I reflect back to when I was young and the young Herb Greenberg is lying here, saying, 'Who the hell am I to go on a cruise?'"

So there's a young Herb Greenberg inside of you who never thought he could possibly go on a cruise?

"Exactly," he says, nodding. "And my cruise back then was the Staten Island Ferry."

It is a time of bringing together the best of the past with the possibilities of the future.

"It is. That's a good way of putting it," he says.

If you don't mind my asking, what is your biggest fear right now?

"There are two fears, really. One is that I won't be able to continue to tolerate the medicine. The other is that as they adjust the medicine so that I can tolerate it better, I won't be getting enough medicine to keep the cancer at bay," he says, then pauses. "You see, I don't want people to feel that I'm in a life-and-death situation right now. I just need to carry on. And beat this thing. I'm certainly *not* prepared to say, the hell with it, I'll just live the remainder of my life as fully as I can for the next 'X' period of time, and then quietly die. That's not me."

Do not go gently into that good night, right?

"No. Absolutely not. I still have much to do." Pausing, he adds, "I want to make sure that Caliper carries on with the same intensity, the same passion, the same zest that I created. And I'd like to make sure that our concepts have more of an impact on people's lives—on making this cockeyed world just a little better."

Advice for a Young Entrepreneur

What advice might you have for someone who asked you what it takes to be an entrepreneur?

"Well, the first thing is money," Herb says, smiling. "It really is a question of *if* they have enough money—at least enough to survive their early, unexpected failures, which are going to be inevitable."

In your case, you borrowed the money.

"Right. However you get it," he says, "you have to be comfortable with owing money. More than you've ever owed before. And realize that

that is the cost of trying to build your own business. The next question is, How tough are you? Can you survive a beating? Of course, I don't mean physically. But can your ego survive the difficulties, rejections, and even failures that are bound to happen?"

How long do you need for your money to last?

"You just never know," he says, shaking his head. "In our case, we borrowed all we could get. But even with three months free rent, we ran out of it very quickly. All I can say for sure is that you need to have as much money as you have moxie." He pauses, then adds, "I'm not trying to be discouraging. It's just what you need to enter the game."

Like a boxer would not enter the ring without expecting to get punched a couple of times?

"Right. You're going to take a beating, financially and emotionally. And the odds are against you. *So you have to be willing to enter a situation where you know that you probably will not make it—while you absolutely believe that you will.* You've got to know somewhere deep inside that you can take it, that you are in it to the end, whenever that may be. You have to know that what you are pursuing is worth it and that it means that much to you. So when you get knocked down, you can pick yourself back up and go at it again. Even though you might lose rounds five and six, a championship bout is 12 rounds. You've got to be willing to lose some of those rounds and still believe that you will win the match. Through all of that, you've got to be willing to bleed."

That's an interesting phrase. To bleed?

"Sure. You're going to bleed," he says. "If you are on the cutting edge, pursing something that you are passionate about, giving it your all because you see that it could be your future, you're going to bleed."

But then all you need are some Band-Aids.

Psychological Insights—Succession

As a leader, one of your most important responsibilities is to develop future leaders within your organization. That starts with being able to recognize someone else's potential—which, in many ways, is like trying to see into the future.

"Recognizing leadership potential goes beyond acknowledging that someone has talent. In fact, potential leaders can often go unnoticed in organizations because they may be typecast in their current role. He or she may be seen as an excellent technician or an admirable manager. But do they have the potential to be a leader?" Herb asked.

Ram Charan, noted author and expert in business strategy, provides an interesting insight: individuals with enormous potential are focused on "their own journey," he says. "Leaders want to take people with them."

"Talent can be hidden," Herb adds, "and sometimes an individual's particular talent can overshadow one of his or her other talents. For instance, I remember when Frank Sinatra first emerged on the scene, everyone was blown away by what a phenomenal singer he was. But people almost laughed at the idea of him being an actor, as well—until he appeared in *From Here to Eternity*."

How can you determine if someone on your team has the potential to lead? And, if they do, what gaps will need to be filled?

"Part of it," Herb says, "starts with having a culture where you believe in identifying and developing talent. We recommend conducting and sharing the insights from in-depth personality profiles, as well as 360 degree analyses, with key employees. This way, they gain a clearer understanding of what really motivates them, how they come across to others, and what they need to do to improve.

"With that background," Herb adds, "we recommend having periodic conversations with people about their goals for the future. Are they interested in moving up? Are they able to see beyond the confines of their current role? Do they bring a perspective on the outside marketplace? Are they able to notice competitive trends? Can they focus on what is really important? Are they interested in developing the talent of others? Can they crystalize the critical action items needed to move forward? Can they create a spirit to make things happen? Such individuals can be extremely valuable to your organization. Believe in them. Recognize them. Promote them. Reward them. Invest in them. Create training programs, coaching, and experiences (such as managing a new project or team) for them. Allow them to take on responsibilities that they would not otherwise—opening them up to their leadership potential."

What is the best way for you, as a leader, to coach someone who you sense has the potential to be a future leader?

"You have to start with a real, honest, and deep connection between both of you. Because that will also be the connection between where your company is now and where it could be in the future," Herb says. "Then the person you are coaching needs to be open, flexible, focused, driven, and have a strong commitment to change. And you need to let them know that you will be there to support and follow-through with them."

He adds, "Coaching, ultimately, is about bridging the gap between understanding and doing. Most coaching is based on a huge, and false, assumption that if people understand, they will do the right thing. But change is never that easy. Coaching is about changing time-honored habits and replacing them with new ones. And habits are difficult to change. Just ask yourself, 'Why do so many people who have had a triple bypass operation, a year later resume their old eating habits?' If we are not going to change when something is life-threatening, then why in the world are we going to change one of our habits at work just because our boss wants us to?

"Change is not easy," Herb says, then quickly adds, "No, let me say it differently. Change is hard. But if the individual you are coaching has an enormous desire, along with the willingness to continually improve, the self-awareness, and the ability to always take two steps forward (even though they will definitely, at times, end up taking one step back), then you can succeed. Leadership development starts with having the right attitude. And, when all is said and done, I believe, the right attitude is worth 50 IQ points.

"The toughest aspect to work on," he adds, "is someone's emotional intelligence. The interpersonal, leadership, and communication skills take time, effort, and a strong desire on the part of the potential leader to want to change, to improve, and to keep getting better and better and better. This is something that has to come from inside them. Deep inside of them."

So as you look to coach and mentor someone for a leadership position, the questions that need to be asked first are: Is the individual you are coaching truly interested in improving? Is he or she flexible? Open? Self-aware? And do they have a strong desire to change? Herb says, "That's who your coaching will stick to. If they are truly interested in reaching out to others and reaching in to themselves, they can change. And, at the end of the day, those are the individuals who have the potential to become your next leaders. They are the individuals who can make the difference to your organization's future."

Questions to Ask Yourself About Your Future

These questions are posed for you to consider as you create
your own vision, tap into your personal strengths, and pursue
your own leadership journey. Your answers to these questions will provide a starting point to consider the role that
your view about the future plays into your approach to leadership. You are encouraged to consider these questions at
different times, as your answers will undoubtedly evolve and
change as your leadership journey unfolds.

1. Do you know the next step in your leadership journey?
2. Do you know who could replace you in your current position?
   Have you been grooming him or her to replace you?
3. Are you ready to let go of your current responsibilities?
4. Are you ready to take on new leadership responsibilities?
5. What appeals to you most about taking on those
   responsibilities?
6. What will you miss most about what you are currently doing?
7. Do you have a trusted advisor?
8. Are you a trusted advisor to someone else?
9. What are your trusted conversations about?

What's Your Story?

Herb's premise has always been to look for that which is not so easily seen—our potential. He found a way to see that potential within us.

Interestingly, for those of us who are sighted, what we see can get in the way of what really is. Sometimes our preconceived notions can color our judgment. Other times, as they say, "Objects in the rearview mirror are closer than they appear."

What Herb intuitively understood, as Bill George shared in his book *True North*, is that the journey of authentic leadership begins with a deep understanding of the story of your life.

In Herb's story, there are certain motifs, certain themes that repeat themselves like the chorus of a song and resonate and connect with force, clarity, and consistency. These themes come alive through stories, helping to define him in ways that he and others can easily connect with, recognize, and admire.

It all starts with a story.

For Herb, of course, his story starts in Brooklyn. From there, the Bridge took him to places he could have never imagined. The Dodgers, the trolley cars, and the street vendors all add color to the story of a young boy growing up with the notion that "there will always be next season." We hear about him losing his sight, and his parents refusing to allow him to be sent away to a school for the blind. We see him with a baseball cap pulled low over his forehead in the Dodger's dugout, and fade to him touching his cheek where Betty Grable kissed him or trading statistics and opinions with Red Barber about their team. We see a close-up of him being beaten up on his way to school, then other bigots attacking him at summer camp. He takes to heart his father's message that he had to be "just a little better" because some people might not give him an equal chance. Fast-forward to him writing his dissertation about people who are disadvantaged, yet not able to get a college teaching position because he is blind. There he is finally teaching in Texas, telling his students that instead of class today, they are all going to listen to history being made as the Brooklyn Dodgers would win their first and only World Series against those damn Yankees. Fade to him discovering a way to assess sales potential, then being told that the company that wanted this assessment has no need for it anymore. We see him on the brink of losing his fledgling company because he could not come up with a single client, then holding his first contract with the Buick Division of General Motors. Now we see him expanding his psychological understanding of what it takes to succeed across all professions and helping welfare recipients find their first jobs, then helping professional sports teams with their draft choices, and finally taking his company international. He empirically proves that women bring to leadership qualities that are ideally conducive to today's global marketplace. He almost loses his company in the Great Recession, then creates a new paradigm, helping his clients develop top talent among their current employees, which puts his company on solid footing for the future. Throughout, we see him openly and honestly reflecting on his accomplishments, doubts, fears, hopes, and dreams, while gazing as far as he can into the future, doing everything in his power to position his company to be carried into the next generation.

Woven into Herb's stories are qualities and values that come forth and themes that connect with each other, creating a consistent and authentic worldview. First, there is the prejudice he encountered and overcame. Then there is his sheer moxie. Coupled with this is his natural connection with anyone who was not given an equal opportunity. Then, of course, he is never quite satisfied, always knowing that there is something more to do. This leads to his fervent belief in wanting to make a difference—his feeling fortunate and wanting to give back. Throughout, there is the constant drive to take a shot at a new opportunity. And that constant drive is always immediate.

These are the themes that reside and resound in Herb's story and that make him so intriguing. Throughout his life, he heard the thunderous sound of unmistakably negative messages, alongside the resoundingly compelling sound of positive messages.

Fortunately, he paid more attention to the positive messages.

Along the way, adhering to those positive messages helped Herb sense opportunities, be provocative, and thoroughly enjoy what he was doing.

In addition to accepting the positive messages, what is equally compelling about Herb's story is that he was never willing to accept the stigma or the limitations of being blind. His unwavering, determined, positive attitude in the face of challenges, adversity, disappointments, and failures is what we marvel at—and find truly inspiring.

As Herb's daughter Holly says so succinctly and so beautifully about her father: "He is this person with all those advanced degrees and all those amazing accomplishments, while, at the same time, my father is still a 10-year-old boy who has just lost his sight." Inside of that seeming paradox is part of what makes Herb and his story so interesting, so deep, and so compelling.

That is why—beyond inspiring you, hopefully Herb's story will also help you see the significance of understanding *your* leadership story and realize how important it is to be able to convey your story in a way that is clear, meaningful, compelling, and authentic.

Your leadership story is what illuminates you, making you known, understood, and worth following. Ultimately, your story defines you as a leader.

Your story expresses who you are. Where are you from? Where are you going? What do you stand for? What will you not stand for?

These are some of the questions you need to answer—convincingly.

To the extent that your life's stories reflect your values, others will lean in and be interested. After all, the fundamental reason others will follow you is because they believe in you, they believe in who you are, and *they believe your story.*

Your leadership story is much more than just a recording or recitation of the facts of your life. It is *your personal narrative.* What is the essence of your story? What are the themes that are important, consistent, and true to you?

Once you know these themes and are able to convey them convincingly, others will listen to your vision, your goals, and your hopes and dreams. First, though, they need to know who you are, that they can trust you, and that you are there for them and always will be.

Getting at the heart of your story starts with knowing the sound of your own heart. It takes deep reflection, coupled with the ability to tell your story in a way that connects your heart with the hearts of others.

To clarify your story, you need to start by asking yourself the kind of questions that Herb did of himself and that others will want to know about you.

What experiences transformed you? What did you learn about yourself by facing a particular challenge? How did you handle your doubts and fears? How have your transformative experiences shaped a consistent pattern in your life? How did those experiences enable you to understand the deeper purpose of your leadership journey? Can you articulate what you have learned about yourself and others in a way that is open, honest, approachable, credible, meaningful, and inspiring?

Keep in mind that while you, no doubt, have heroes and, hopefully, mentors, your story is not about them. Your story is no one else's but your own. Others have certainly influenced you, but this is not the time for emulation or imitation. This is the time for you to be honest and real. This is where you open up. No one wants to follow an impersonator. What people are looking for is you. As a leader, people need you to be clear about and demonstrate a passion for your purpose. They want to know that you practice your values consistently. And they absolutely want to know that you lead from your heart as well as your head. People are not looking for you to say the perfect words. They are looking for you to show up, being absolutely real and believable. They are seeking to believe

This is not an easy process. Developing your leadership story will not happen overnight. There are many approaches you can use to help develop and refine your leadership story—including self-reflection, meditating, journaling, asking the right questions, and sharing your insights and stories with your high-quality connections.

You might find that an easier place for you to enter this journey is to consider the key qualities and values that are consistent throughout your life. Is it your perseverance? Your courage? Your self-awareness? Your resilience? Your optimism? Your empathy? Your competitiveness? Your willingness to take a risk? Your persuasiveness? Your confidence? Your passion? Your integrity? Your creativity?

Consider which quality you personify at your very best. Getting clear about your foundational qualities and values will help you understand who you are at your very core.

With that clarity and understanding, you can start to weave together the transformative stories that have helped define you. Why did you take one road rather than the other? Can you describe the transformative effects of a personal or professional loss? Was there a challenge that you rose above, and in that rising, discovered your true purpose and passion? These are the stories that get at the heart of who you are as a leader.

Keep this in mind as you consider some of your favorite, most memorable and formative experiences. When have you felt you were most yourself? Or when did you wish you were more of yourself? How did certain experiences express your core values and your key qualities? What did you learn about yourself from those experiences? How have you changed?

The answers to those questions will start to create the narrative for your leadership story. Authentic leaders, as Bill George underscores, are able to trace their inspiration directly from their life stories. Then, as Herminia Ibarra, professor at INSEAD and the author of *Working Identity*, says, your story can provide the inspiration for others to create their own futures.

Those who will want to follow you are also looking for what psychologist Erik Erikson called *generativity*, or the ability to look beyond your own immediate future to something that is bigger than yourself. In his book *The Life Cycle Completed*, Erikson notes that after fusing a sense of identity and establishing long-term intimacy bonds, we are all looking for our leaders to nurture, teach, lead, and promote the next generation.

To the extent that you can frame your own story as connecting your past with a present and future that engages our hopes and dreams, you can position yourself as a leader worth following. Others want to hear your stories—resulting from key events from your past, fused with a clear perception of the present and an inspiring view that makes us anticipate the future. That is what will define your leadership identity. As Dan McAdams, professor at Northwestern University and the author of *Stories We Live By*, says, "Through our personal myths, each of us discovers what is true and what is meaningful in life."

When all is said and done, we become engaged when we hear stories about individuals who have overcome adversity and transformed themselves, learning something about themselves and carrying on with a positive attitude that we can only admire and wish to emulate. We cannot help but wonder if we could do the same in those circumstances. And inside of that wondering, a connection is formed. Within that inspiration is where the leadership journey can begin.

Ultimately, the message is, if you are intent on becoming a leader, you have to start by being clear about who you are, so that others can have that same clarity and be compelled to follow your lead.

Most significantly, you will find that as your story unfolds, you will gain insights and clarity into your values—and how you have lived them. You will know what is really important to you and what qualities in you come out when you are at your best. Once you are clear on the values and qualities that are core to your beliefs, and how your experiences have challenged those values and qualities, you will know what you are made of. Then you will become ready to tell your leadership story. And with that story, you will be able to connect with others in ways that were previously unimagined.

At the end of the day, what you want to do, as Herb did so very well, is to identify how your personal stories connect who you are in the most direct way to your core values and your key qualities. That connection is where your leadership journey will take shape. Inside of those stories is where a deep realization will take form (for you and for others) of the leader you were always intended to become.

Then, as Herb notes, "Others will follow you because they sense that you are genuine, they know who you are, and they can believe in you." What they need to know, in order to follow you, is that you care about them; that you are real, open, honest, and insightful; and that, together, you are ready to help them discover a new future.

Are You Seeing Clearly?

As you hone your unique leadership strengths and shape your personal leadership story, you will begin to get a clearer sense of how your experiences and aspirations connect.

And you will start to see yourself and the world around you differently.

In some ways, it might seem like an annual eye examination. As lenses are quickly switched in front of you, through a process of elimination, you will decide which lenses help you see slightly better than all the rest.

Is this clearer? How about this? How is this one? Is this any better?

This is how you can clarify your personal vision. Only this time, you are looking inside—as if simultaneously seeing your past, your present, and your future.

Start by eliminating the lenses that no longer work for you. Then focus on what does work for you.

Are you looking at life the way you always have? Are you adjusting your outlook? Are things a little blurry? Getting clearer?

It is the ideal time to have some real and honest conversations with yourself. Then with those you trust. Are they seeing things the way you are? Or slightly differently? Those conversations can help to bring your leadership story—and your vision of yourself—into focus.

Then reflect. It is a time for looking deeply inside, then widely outside. It is a time to look at what is and what can be. It is the perfect time to see clearly a world of new possibilities unfolding before your eyes.

Psychological Insights—Looking Within

Being a leader is about continually evolving. It is not a one-time deal. It is not just a place where you arrive. And it is often not for all time.

Some leaders are ideal at harnessing the excitement of the early stages of a start-up. Others are better at creating new standards, systems, and operational procedures as a company grows and becomes more complex. It takes a different kind of leader to go head-to-head with one huge competitor. And it takes yet another kind of leader to take a company through its most trying time.

Winston Churchill was the ideal leader to inspire and rally the British people during World War II. But his leadership skills were not what was needed to organize the country's rebuilding after the war.

"We each bring unique strengths to different situations," Herb says. "There can be elements of leadership in many jobs, as in many aspects of life. The key is to allow the leader within you to be expressed fully."

As you pursue your leadership journey, some questions you will need to keep exploring are: Are you aware of your strengths? And your limitations? Are you able to connect with others and elevate *their* sense of who they can be and what we all can be? Are you facing a situation that brings out the best in you? Are you ready to be tested in ways you never have before? Is this your time to lead?

As Daniel Goleman points out in his book *Primal Leadership*, there is a new yardstick for measuring your effectiveness as a leader. "The new measure takes for granted having enough intellectual ability and technical know-how. . . . It focuses instead on personal qualities, such as initiative and empathy, adaptability and persuasiveness."

Our emotional intelligence, Goleman notes, is based on five elements: self-awareness, motivation, self-regulation, empathy, and adeptness in relationships. And the importance of emotional intelligence, he has found, increases the higher you go in an organization. In fact, he notes, intellectual and technical superiority play absolutely no role in leadership success. His studies show that at the top executive levels, everyone needs high-level cognitive skills, but being better at them does not make a star leader. Rather, according to his studies, emotional intelligence accounts for close to 90 percent of leadership success.

"To be an emotionally intelligent leader," Herb underscores, "you need to start with a strong sense of your own self-worth and a belief in your own capabilities. You also need to be keenly aware of your own emotions and their effect on others. And you need to have an honest understanding of your own strengths and limitations. Meanwhile, your empathy will help you sense others' feelings and perspectives, while genuinely caring about developing them and bolstering their abilities."

Herb adds, "To follow you, others need to know two things. First they need to know that you care about them, that you are in it for them. Then they need to know that they can trust you, that you are honest and have integrity." He adds, "When they are sure that they can trust you and that you care about them, they will be open to your initiative, creativity, and drive to achieve. Then they will look to you to inspire and guide them, to listen openly, to convey compelling messages about what is going on and what will be, to manage conflict, to initiate and manage change, and to develop innovative teams."

As a leader, no one is looking for you to score 100 on all of those responsibilities. But they are looking for you to score very high on most of them. And to be genuinely, rigorously, and continually trying to improve on all of the others.

Are you ready to keep getting ready?

Questions to Ask Yourself About Your Story

These questions are posed for you to consider as you create your own vision, tap into your personal strengths, and pursue your own leadership journey. Your answers to these questions will provide a starting point to consider how your personal story is the basis of your leadership journey. You are encouraged to consider these questions at different times, as your answers will undoubtedly evolve and change as your leadership journey unfolds.

1. When you encounter a problem, what is the first thing you look for?
2. When you encounter an opportunity, what is the first thing you look for?
3. What are you *not* seeing?
4. As a leader, what do you bring to the table that no one else does quite as well?
5. What do you absolutely love doing? What does it feel like when you are doing what you absolutely love? How could you do more of it?
6. What is your definition of success?
7. How has your definition of success changed throughout the years? Are you ready to change it again?
8. Are you realizing your potential?
9. What would you like a child to learn from your life?
10. How will you lead differently today than you did yesterday?
11. What do you want to do tomorrow?
12. What do you want to do for the rest of your life?

There Is a Light Within You

There is a light that comes from you, and it can connect with all of us.

Your light is meant to shine. By knowing that it is your time, you can help create the best of times. You can also make your time a little lighter and a little brighter.

Realize that this is *your* time. It is your time to be here. Now. Shining like a star. Don't miss it. Don't be elsewhere. Reset your internal watch for *now*.

A bright light shines, within and around you, on the time that is yours. It is now.

Shine on.

Conclusion: Your Next Step

As a gift to you, Herb would like to provide you with a way to get some objective insights into the qualities that drive and distinguish you. Consider this to be Herb's contribution to your leadership journey.

Herb is offering you the opportunity to take Caliper's online, in-depth personality profile, which is the same assessment used by Fortune 500 companies and thousands of midsized and small companies around the world to assess the potential of their applicants and employees.

You are welcome to take this assessment at no cost and receive a written report pinpointing the qualities that differentiate you.

This Developmental Guide will provide you with some interesting and valuable insights, highlighting some of your key strengths and motivations, along with suggestions for developing your potential.

If you are a leader or seeking to become one, the results can also help you understand how you connect with others, as you consider how you might think about yourself and the individuals in your organization differently.

To take advantage of your free online assessment, go to: WhatYou ArentSeeing.com. Enter your access code: 012345. Then follow the directions.

Of course, if you are interested in coaching, Caliper's consultants are always available to you. They can provide you with guidance in hiring, developing, team building, succession planning, and organizational development. Just visit Caliper's website: Calipercorp.com.

The next steps on your leadership journey are all yours. Consider the results of your online personality assessment. Reflect on the parts of Herb's story in this book that resonate with you most strongly. Keep asking yourself those challenging introspective questions. Talk with friends and colleagues about what you are considering. Your inner compass will guide you as your road map comes into focus. You have known the direction all along. The destination is yours. Shine on.

Acknowledgments

First and foremost, I want to thank Mary Glenn, associate publisher, and Cheryl Ringer, associate editor, at McGraw-Hill, who, with enthusiasm and confidence, encouraged me to explore and expand the initial concept for this book. Together, Mary and Cheryl offered wonderful insights, suggestions, and encouragement that deepened my thoughts and feelings about what was possible.

My heartfelt thanks go to Herb for being so open and forthcoming about sharing his successes, challenges, failures, and everything in between, providing an inspiring story with unique experiences, reflections, and lessons from which we can all continually learn.

I also want to thank Thomas Schoenfelder, Caliper's senior vice president of research and development, who joined me on many of the interviews I conducted with Herb, enriching the conversations and offering valuable insights. My eternal gratitude also goes to Ramona Rettzo, who transcribed nearly 100 hours of interviews with Herb, his family members, colleagues, and clients. These recordings were managed by a team at Caliper that included Amy Yates-Wuelfing, Agota Alvarez, Sandra Vengels, Stephanie Zimmerman, Kathy Berry, and Christine Briegs.

Most significantly, as always, I thank my wife Donna for touching my heart, for believing in what can be, for her uncanny way of listening so clearly, for her deeply inspired messages, for her warm smile, for the light in her eyes, for the sound of her laughter, and for opening new possibilities.

Index